GRACE ALONE

TEN SERMONS

BY

JOHN KERSHAW
of ROCHDALE

With Foreword by K. W. H. Howard

Published by and obtainable from
ZOAR PUBLICATIONS
44 Queen's Drive, Ossett. W. Yorks., WF5 0ND
England

1976

ISBN 0 904435 09 1

Printed in England by
Oldham & Manton Ltd.
1 Rugby Street, Leicester, LE3 5FF

CONTENTS

FOREWORD

John Kershaw was a Lancashire preacher of some eminence during the middle half of the nineteenth century. He travelled constantly in an area bounded in the west by Preston, Bolton and Manchester; and in the east by Keighley, Leeds and Barnsley. Occasionally he also visited the English midlands, the west country, and London. Wherever he went the blessing of God attended his ministry in remarkable ways. Such a record alone might be regarded as enough for any one man; yet this man was also the faithful, devoted, and beloved pastor of a large congregation at Hope Chapel, Rochdale, for fifty-two years.

Born in Rochdale in 1792, Kershaw died in the same place in 1870, respected by the entire community, highly esteemed by churchmen and dissenters alike for his gracious consistency of character and for his works' sake, and all but revered by the flock over which the Holy Ghost had made him an overseer. The story of his conversion and call by grace, his call to the ministry, and his busy and fruitful life, is told in an arresting and instructive manner in his oft-reprinted *Autobiography*.

The printed page can never fully convey the living speech of a christian minister; nor can it register anything of the spiritual unction attending the preached word. But this is the best that can be done with regard to preachers of Kershaw's day. This is the first published volume of his sermons. *Grace Alone* is its title because though it presents a variety of subjects grace alone is its dominant theme. It may be wondered what relevance this selection of nineteenth century sermons has to the contemporary religious scene. Three points may be made by way of response.

(i). It is still ignorantly argued that free grace religion is a religion of the head only, arid and barren, dry and heartless. Such critics will do well to read Kershaw on "Seeing Jesus" and, "Immutability". Having done so, let them ask what their own hearts know of his intense affection for the person of the Lord Jesus Christ, his struggle to find superlatives enough to exalt his all-blessed Saviour, and his consuming passion that his hearers also should —

'John in the everlasting song,
And crown him Lord of all.'

(ii). This is a day of pathetically short and sadly ineffective pastorates in every branch of evangelical christendom. Lifetime pastorates, with the rarest exceptions, are a thing of the past. In Kershaw's day a pastor was often regarded as married to his people, and the 'till death do us part' element was a most happy ingredient in the pastoral bond. When Kershaw had been 'married' to his flock in Rochdale for fifty years he preached by way of jubilee the sermon, 'Finishing our Course with Joy'. It displays a balance of concern that he should himself be kept faithful to the end, and an unwearied pastoral vigilance for the spiritual well-being of his people. Free grace religion and pastoral affection and obeying "them that have the rule over you" belong together!

(iii). There is a widespread notion that the distinctive doctrines of sovereign grace may be held but ought not to be preached, because the people do not understand and cannot receive them. How, then, it may be asked, will they ever receive what is never preached to them? In 1834 Kershaw spent several weeks among a congregation of ordinary countryfolk in Wiltshire. He preached three sermons on the distinctive doctrines of salvation by grace alone. When the final service was ended the entire congregation rose and with upheld hands besought him to print the sermons that they might be of permanent benefit to themselves and to the Church of God. Kershaw had preached from the heart. Later he wrote, 'In complying with your request, I have had to trust to the Lord and the memory He has given me, as I had no notes to guide me.' The result was the minor classic on the faithfulness and longsuffering of God with which this selection closes.

The Author's Preface was in fact part of Kershaw's preface to 'Faithfulness and Longsuffering' dated from Hope Chapel, Rochdale, Jan. 5, 1835. It is placed at this point because it displays his honest and forthright character, and because it stresses the theme of the whole volume — *Grace Alone.*

May the God of all grace make great grace abound to His people, bestow saving grace on sinners far and near, and magnify His own great Name, to the praise of the glory of His grace.

Stamford, 1976   K. W. H. Howard

AUTHOR'S PREFACE

My prayer is that the reading of these sermons may prove to be to many what the preaching of them did — the savour of life unto life to them that are saved, and of death unto death to them that perish; that they may be as God's mouth separating the precious from the vile. "He that hath my word, let him speak my word faithfully. What is the chaff to the wheat? saith the LORD." (Jer. 23. 28.)

It is a lamentable fact that many who profess to believe the distinguishing doctrines of grace either keep them entirely in the background, or if they do speak of them, it is in so distant and indefinite a manner that their hearers must be very quick at hearing if they can tell what is piped or what is harped (1 Cor. 14. 7); and this is done for fear of giving offence to those who cannot endure sound doctrine. Is this following the example of the great Prophet of the Church, who when He entered into the synagogue, read that part of the prophecy of Isaiah which says, "The spirit of the Lord GOD is upon me; because he hath anointed me to preach the Gospel to the poor. . ."? And when He had closed the book, the eyes of all them that were in the synagogue were fastened on Him, and they wondered at the gracious words which proceeded out of His mouth. But this preacher, who spake as never man spake, was He that searches hearts and tries the reins, and He knew that His hearers could not endure sound doctrine. Therefore, to make this manifest, He said, "But I tell you of a truth, many widows were in Israel in the days of Elias, when the heaven was shut up three years and six months, when great famine was throughout all the land; but unto none of them was Elias sent, save unto Sarepta, a city of Sidon, unto a woman that was a widow. And many lepers were in Israel, in the time of Eliseus the prophet; and none of them was cleansed, saving Naaman the Syrian." Now this He said unto them, that it might be made manifest that they loved neither Him nor His doctrine; for they understood by it that "the Lord had mercy on whom he would have mercy," and this they did not like: as it is written, "And all they in the synagogue, when they heard these things, were filled with wrath, and rose up, and thrust him out of the city, and led him unto the brow of the hill whereon their city was built, that they might cast him down headlong. But he, passing through the midst of them, went his way." (Luke 4. 16-30.)

On another occasion, our Lord fed a great multitude with five barley loaves and two small fishes; and many followed Him, and professed to be His disciples, "because they did eat of the loaves and were filled." But our Lord, knowing that they did not love Him, nor His blessed truth, said to them, "All that the Father giveth me shall come to me, and him that cometh to me I will in no wise cast out. . . . No man can come to me except the Father which hath sent me draw him; and I will raise him up at the last day. . . . Except ye eat the flesh of the Son of man, and drink his blood, ye have no life in you. And he that eateth this bread shall live for ever. . . . Many therefore of his (professed) disciples, when they heard this, said, This is an hard saying; who can hear it?" One said, I neither can nor will hear it; and another said, If this be the doctrine He preaches, they may hear Him that will. Therefore, "from that time many of his disciples went back and walked no more with him."

And so it would be in the present day, were Christ to make His appearance again in the same humble circumstances, having a few poor illiterate fishermen for His disciples, preaching the same pride-abasing and God-glorifying truth. Many who are now crying, "Hosannah to the Lord," would be like the professed disciples of old, ready to turn their back upon Him, and would cry out, "Crucify him, crucify him! for it is not fit that such a fellow should live." Our Lord, seeing these disciples go back, said unto the twelve, "Will ye also go away?" Peter answered him, "Lord, to whom shall we go? thou hast the words of eternal life." (John 6. 26-68).

The true disciples of Christ follow Him as a matter of necessity. They see an end of perfection in themselves, because God's law is exceeding broad, and all refuges but Christ they find to be refuges of lies. They are led by the Holy Spirit to say, as Peter said on another occasion, "Neither is there salvation in any other; for there is none other name under heaven given among men, whereby we must be saved;" and they cleave to the Lord with full purpose of heart. Like Paul, they are determined to know nothing but Christ Jesus and Him crucified; for it is the glory of the true Christian to be nothing and less than nothing and vanity in himself that Christ may be his all in all.

John Kershaw

1

The Rock of Salvation

PREACHED AT ZOAR CHAPEL, GREAT ALIE ST., LONDON,
ON LORDS DAY EVENING, APRIL 30, 1848.

*"The LORD liveth; and blessed be my rock; and let the God of
my salvation be exalted." (Psalm 18. 46).*

The gracious words of our text set forth the glorious Person
of our Lord Jesus Christ, concerning whom the Apostle says, as
it can be said of no other, that He is "Jesus Christ the same
yesterday, and to-day, and for ever" (Heb. 13. 8.) All things in
nature and in providence change. The feelings and exercises of
the christian mind are ever numerous and changing. But
whatever takes place in nations, in churches, in families, or in
the feelings of our minds, "the LORD liveth; and blessed be our
rock," (the Rock of Ages, for He never moves!) "and let the
God of my salvation be exalted."

These words have been a great comfort and support to my
mind in trials and in bereavements. For whoever stands or falls
in a profession of religion; whoever goes or comes, lives or
dies, "The Lord liveth"!

It has fallen to my lot since I have been a pastor over a
Christian church, to commit many of my near, dear, and choice
friends, with whom I have walked together in sweet company
in the fear of the Lord and in the comfort of the Holy Ghost
for many years, to the silent tomb. Such bereavements cannot

but be keenly felt, though our loss is the eternal gain of our departed brethren and sisters in the Lord. But when choice friends die to us in this world, these words have soothed and comforted my mind many times — my Lord and Master lives! Yes; bless His name, the Lord lives! Jesus is the same; He never dies! "What man is he that liveth, and shall not see death?" But, blessed be our Rock; He never dies, He lives for ever!

Our text divides itself into three parts. *First, "The LORD liveth." Secondly, "Blessed be my Rock,"* and *Thirdly, the exaltation of the God of our salvation.*

I. — In the *first* place, *"The LORD liveth."* This is our Lord Jesus Christ, the immortal Word — He who created the heavens and the earth; He who in the Book of The Revelation calls Himself the Alpha and Omega, the beginning and the ending, the first and the last; which is, and which was, and which is to come, the Almighty. He who is the maker of all things visible and invisible. He who was made flesh and dwelt among us, and manifested His glory as of the only begotten of the Father full of grace and truth. He who veiled his Godhead in a clay tabernacle and condescended to be "made of a woman, made under the law, to redeem them that were under the law."

This brings us to what Paul calls "the mystery of godliness." He says, "without controversy great is the mystery of godliness: God was manifest in the flesh, justified in the Spirit, seen of angels, preached unto the Gentiles, believed on in the world, received up to glory." (1 Tim. 3. 16.) There was absolute necessity for the Immortal Word to assume our nature without sin in the womb of the Virgin, that in that nature He might bear all our transgressions away, die for our iniquities, and shed His precious blood for the remission of our sins; that sin might be condemned in His flesh; that is, in the holy soul and body of the immaculate Jesus. Paul says, "For what the law could not do, in that it was weak through the flesh, God sending his own Son in the likeness of sinful flesh, and for sin, condemned sin in the flesh." (Rom. 8. 3.) "Christ died for our sins according to the scriptures." (1 Cor. 15. 3) The awful and solemn death of Jesus, His crucifixion and blood-shedding, is the pillar of the christian religion, and the grand foundation of the church of God. The sinner who is awakened to see and feel his lost, ruined, and undone state; to behold the inflexible holiness and justice of God, and brought at the same time to feel himself sinking within under the terrors of God in a broken law — that poor guilty, sin-condemned wretch, has nowhere else to look for peace, comfort, or rest, but to the Lord Jesus Christ. He died for our sins. He "was delivered for our offences, and raised again for our justification."

Now this is the very gospel the apostle Paul preached; therefore he lays such emphasis upon it in that memorable chapter, 1 Cor. 15. Let me read a few verses of it. He says, "Moreover, brethren, I declare unto you the gospel which I preached unto you, which also ye have received, and wherein ye stand: by which also ye are saved, if ye keep in memory what I preached unto you, unless ye have believed in vain. For I delivered unto you first of all that which I also received, how that Christ died for our sins according to the scriptures: and that he was buried, and that he rose again the third day according to the scriptures." (vv. 1-3) The solemn and awful death of Jesus, the incarnate God: His blood-shedding for the remission of our sins, and His resurrection from the dead, is the foundation upon which God's church is raised for eternity.

But the Lord of glory who was crucified and slain for our sins, now lives! He was "declared to be the Son of God with power, according to the spirit of holiness, by his resurrection from the dead." (Rom. 1. 4.) Or, as Peter says, on the day of Pentecost, "Whom God hath raised up, having loosed the pains of death; because it was not possible that he should be holden of it." (Acts. 2. 24.) But why could not death and hell hold the Redeemer fast? For this very blessed and obvious reason. He bore the sin of His church in His own body on the tree, and cast it for ever into the depths of the sea; He endured the tremendous penalty due to transgression, and delivered His church and people by being made a curse for them; He satisfied law and justice; He wrought out and brought in an everlasting righteousness; He spoiled principalities and powers; and conquered death, and him that had the power of it, that is, the Devil! Christ took the sting of death away; and therefore He could not be held fast by it. He triumphed gloriously over Satan's territory in His resurrection from the dead. He was the plague of death, and the destruction of the powers of darkness.

Our Jesus lives! Though He died, He rose again the third day according to the scriptures. I must quote that chapter again. Paul says, "He was seen of Cephas, then of the twelve: after that, he was seen of above five hundred brethren at once; of whom the greater part remain unto this present, but some are fallen asleep: after that he was seen of James; then of all the apostles: and last of all he was seen of me also, as of one born out of due time." (vv. 4-8) The disciples were witnesses of the death of the Lord Jesus Christ; they saw the mighty miracles that accompanied it; they beheld Him laid in the sepulchre; and they were witnesses also of His resurrection from the dead. Jesus appeared likewise to the women after His resurrection in the garden. He made Himself known also to the two as they journeyed from Emmaus. He appeared to the disciples again when the doors were shut where they were assembled for fear of the Jews, and warmed their hearts while they were conversing about their Lord and Master. And when He gave His disciples their credentials, commanding them not to depart from Jerusalem but wait for the promise of the Father, while He is speaking to them He is taken up to heaven, and a cloud receives Him out of their sight. (Acts 1. 1-9.) Having led captivity captive, the everlasting gates are flung open, and Christ ascends to glory, and takes His seat on high at the right hand of the Majesty above as the great High Priest, Head, and Representative of His people. There, as the exalted Mediator and living Advocate of His redeemed, He ever lives and reigns in immortal glory in the high court of heaven. He is there as the head of His body the church; and He says to all His members on earth, "Because I live, ye shall live also." As sure as Christ the head is in glory, so sure shall every elect vessel of mercy whom He has raised from a death of sin to a life of faith, rise to live with Him in immortal bliss and blessedness for ever and ever. Yes; bless His precious name, "The Lord lives!" He not only lives as the head and representative of His people in the high court of heaven, but He lives there to manage all their affairs.

Now this was the glorious foundation which the apostle Paul laid in his preaching, and it was his support under all his trials — the blood-shedding, death, resurrection, and ascension of the Lord Jesus Christ our great High Priest into heaven. Mark his language; he says, "Who shall lay any thing to the charge of God's elect?" What a solemn and important question this is! Then he adds, "It is Christ that died, yea rather, that is risen again, who is even at the right hand of God, who also maketh intercession for us." (Rom. 8. 33, 34.) Do you not see what a prominent feature the death of Christ has in this solemn question? He lives and intercedes for His redeemed; He pleads their cause, and manages their affairs. The Apostle's soul being fired with these important truths, exclaims in another place, "Wherefore he is able also to save them to the uttermost that come unto God by him, seeing he ever liveth to make intercession for them." (Heb. 7. 25.) Sometimes when I have heard our people singing the following hymn, it has so lifted up my heart and soul that I have scarcely been able to constrain my feelings:—

> Who shall the Lord's elect condemn?
>   'Tis God that justifies their souls:
> And mercy, like a mighty stream,
>   O'er all their sins divinely rolls.
>
> Who shall adjudge the saints to hell?
>   'Tis Christ that suffered in their stead;
> And the salvation to fulfil,
>   Behold Him rising from the dead.
>
> He lives! he lives! and sits above,
>   For ever interceding there;
> Who shall divide us from his love?
>   O, what should tempt us to despair? (Watts)

He ever lives within the veil to plead the cause of His people, and we shall never be disappointed.

"The LORD liveth; and blessed be my rock; and let the God of my salvation be exalted." He lives in heaven; He lives and dwells on earth too. But where is it that He lives and dwells in this world of sin and woe?

1. *The Lord lives in the heart* of every elect vessel of mercy, redeemed by blood, and regenerated by the Spirit. Such a precious soul as this is the palace of the great King, the dwelling-place of the mighty God of Jacob. In the prophecy of Isaiah, we have a beautiful description of the greatness of the exaltation, majesty and glory, and yet at the same time amazing humility and condescension of the Lord of hosts: "For thus saith the high and lofty One that inhabiteth eternity." Let us pause here for a moment. "That inhabiteth eternity!" Eternity is His dwelling-place. You and I inhabit our houses in our short span of existence but for a very little time. But our God, the Rock that is to be exalted, inhabits eternity; "Whose name

is Holy; I dwell in the high and holy place." Heaven is His throne, and the earth is His footstool. He dwells in another place also; "with him that is of a contrite and humble spirit, to revive the spirit of the humble, and to revive the heart of the contrite ones." (Is. 57. 15.) The Lord lives, in the heart of every broken-hearted sinner. He has taken up His abode there; and says, "Here will I dwell for ever, for I have desired it."

Hear the Apostle Paul's heart-cheering testimony in reference to his own case. He says, "I am crucified with Christ; nevertheless I live; yet not I, but Christ liveth in me." You see, Christ lives in the very heart and soul of His people. "And the life which I now live in the flesh I live by the faith of the Son of God, who loved me and gave himself for me." (Gal. 2. 20.) This is doctrine, and good doctrine too. But, as I am speaking these words, and proving them from the Bible, methinks I hear some child of God saying, 'Can ever the Lord Jesus Christ dwell in such a filthy, vile, and evil heart as mine? If he dwells in the heart of His people, I am afraid I never can be one of them. Such a polluted wretch as I am, sure He never can dwell in me." But what this soul says is only a confirmation that the Lord does dwell in His heart. Mark it, then, for your encouragement; it is only such tempted and tried souls as yours that feel their vileness, pollution, helplessness, and weakness. The Lord does not dwell with those who care nothing about sin, who have never had a heart broken on account of their iniquities. O no; the dwelling-place of the Lord Jesus Christ is with the humble, broken, and contrite heart. The haughty looks of man must be brought down, and the Lord of hosts alone exalted in his soul.

"The LORD liveth; and blessed be my rock; and let the God of my salvation be exalted." He lives, then, in the souls of His people. He lives in their prayers, He lives in their praises, He lives in their hearing; yes, He lives in them as their all in all. There is no spiritual life but what is in the Lord Jesus Christ. We are said to be dead, and our "life is hid with Christ in God. When Christ who is our life, shall appear, then shall ye also appear with him in glory." (Col. 3. 3, 4.) So the Lord lives in the hearts of his people.

2. *The Lord lives in the assemblies of His saints.* Wherever His twos and threes are gathered together in His name, there He lives and there he dwells. He says, "In all places where I record my name I will come unto thee, and I will bless

thee." (Ex. 20. 24.) How amazingly the omniscience of the God-head shines forth in this blessed passage of scripture! In this great city, there are now at this present time many gospel churches assembled, through the length and breadth of the land, where the name of the Lord is recorded, where the silver trumpet is being blown, and where the shout of a king is heard in their midst. The Lord comes and lives and dwells in these assemblies. He alone must be exalted in the pulpit, and in the souls of His living people. And as the Lord lives in them, so they live in Him by virtue of their union to Him, and shall never be brought into condemnation. As sure as the Lord now lives in heaven for His people, so shall they live and reign with him in blessedness for ever when time is no more.

II.— I come to the *second* point of our subject, *"Blessed be our rock."* Now who is this Rock? It can be none other than our Lord Jesus Christ. He is in scripture set forth by the character of a rock. But why is this? Because there is nothing so firm and imperishable as a rock. He is exalted by this metaphor to show His immovability and durability.

Let us make a few observations to show wherein the Lord Jesus Christ is a Rock.

1. As a Rock He is *a foundation* to build upon; and the man made wise unto salvation builds his house upon it. This is that glorious Rock spoken of by the Prophet Isaiah, "Behold," says God, "I lay in Zion for a foundation a stone, a tried stone, a precious corner stone, a sure foundation." (Is. 28. 16.) The Apostle Paul taking up the same subject, says, "Other foundation can no man lay than that is laid, which is Jesus Christ." (1 Cor. 3. 11.) The foundation which our God has laid in Zion, and which every Christian minister should lay in his preaching, is the Lord Jesus Christ. Christ in His covenant engagements; Christ in the complexity of His character as God and man; Christ in His pure and holy humanity; Christ in His atoning sacrifice; Christ in His perfect obedience to the divine law; Christ as the living Advocate before the throne — are the themes upon which the minister should dwell. Jesus Christ is the foundation upon which God builds His church for time and for eternity. "On this rock," He says, "I will build my church; and the gates of hell shall not prevail against it." (Matt. 16. 18.) Christ is a rock; and as Rock He is the foundation of the church.

But the text says, "Blessed be our rock." Now a word or two in reference to the blessedness of this Rock. When David was sinking in his feelings in the mud and mire of the slough of despondency he was afraid his feet were not upon this Rock. Bunyan says, 'There are many persons who make a bridge over this slough' But that is not the right way. The Lord's people are brought to feel their sin, their guilt, their burden; they are made to sigh and to cry and to wait patiently till the Lord inclines His ear unto them; and then at last they will say as the Psalmist did, "He brought me up out of an horrible pit, out of the miry clay, and set my feet upon a rock, and established my goings." (Ps. 40. 1, 2.) David could not say by his own wisdom and strength, 'Here is a rock, a firm rock; I will stand upon it for life.' He could not put himself on the rock; he was sinking in the horrible pit, and his feet sticking fast in the mud. But when by the Holy Spirit's witness in his heart, he could feelingly say the Lord had brought him up out of the horrible pit, had set his feet upon the rock, and established his goings — that he was standing for eternity on the incarnate God, on the finished salvation of Christ — that his sins were put away, and he was delivered from the curse of a broken law — that justice was satisfied and heaven opened up through the new and living way; — then feeling the firmness and blessedness of the Rock, he has a song of praise and thanksgiving put into his mouth and his heart. Isaiah says, "Let the inhabitants of the rock sing, let them shout from the top of the mountains." (Is. 42. 11.) The child of God sings and shouts when he sees and feels the blessedness and security of his salvation. If we are built upon this Rock, we shall be found safe in life, safe in death, and safe in the judgment day. There is no safety anywhere else. "The LORD liveth; and blessed be my rock; and let the God of my salvation be exalted."

2.   But again. "Blessed be my Rock." The Lord Jesus Christ is not only a foundation; He is also *the shadow of a great rock in a weary land*. The Prophet Isaiah says, "A man shall be as an hiding-place from the wind, and a covert from the tempest; as rivers of water in a dry place, as the shadow of a great rock in a weary land." (Isa. 32. 2.) We are in the wilderness, in a waste howling desert; this world to a heaven-born soul is a weary land. We sometimes sing,

"Lord what a wretched land is this,
    That yields us no supply:
No cheering fruits, nor wholesome trees,
    Nor streams of living joy."

But there is something more weary than the land we live in. If we look into our hearts, we shall find more weariness there than in all things else around us. Weary of sin, weary of self — where is the poor soul to go? where is he to flee? He can go nowhere but to the Rock of Ages! David says, "When my heart is overwhelmed; lead me to the rock that is higher than I." 'Lead me to Christ — the shadow of a great rock in a weary land. Let me sit down beneath His shade, and enjoy sweet peace, rest, and comfort to my soul.' Ah, this Rock shades us from the fiery flames of Mount Sinai; it shades us from the buffetings of Satan; and oftentimes it shades us in the storms and tempests of life. Sometimes the child of God in this weary land is enabled to sit down by faith sheltered beneath the shadow of this great Rock, and enjoy sweet peace, rest, and communion with the Lord. O how sweet and happy are his feelings then! "The LORD liveth; and blessed be my rock, and let the God of my salvation be exalted."

3. We observe again, in reference to this blessed Rock, the Lord Jesus Christ is not only the shadow of a great Rock in a weary land; but there flows *a stream of water* from this rock to satiate the thirst of His dear people in this barren land. This was beautifully typified by the rock smitten at Horeb. The Apostle says, "The Rock was Christ." There flowed from it a stream which followed the children of Israel in all their wanderings through the wilderness to nourish and refresh them. And so the fountain of precious blood and water that flowed from Immanuel's side follows the church of God through this weary land for the taking away of sin and uncleanness, and for giving sweet comfort and rest to the weary soul. Whenever, by the bedewing influences of the Spirit of God, it enters into their heart and conscience, it fills them with all joy and peace in believing. "Blessed be our Rock," then, for His atoning blood and His justifying righteousness to His

beloved church and people. Well may they say, "The LORD
liveth; and blessed be our rock; and let the God of our
salvation be exalted."

   4.   "Blessed be our rock." There is a cleft in this rock; and
God puts His people in *"the cleft of the rock."*Moses besought
the Lord to show him His glory. But the Lord answered him,
"Thou canst not see my face; for there shall no man see me,
and live." But He said, "Behold there is a place by me, and
thou shalt stand upon a rock." 'Here is a Rock by me, one
brought up with me; on this Rock thou shalt stand and see my
glory.' "And it shall come to pass, while my glory passeth by,
that I will put thee in a clift of the rock, and will cover thee
with my hand while I pass by; and I will take away my hand,
and thou shalt see my back parts; but my face shalt not be
seen." (Ex. 33. 20-23). The Lord put Moses in the cleft of the
rock while He passed by, and displayed His glory and majesty;
and He covered him with His hand of mercy and compassion
while He proclaimed His great and glorious name, as The Lord
God, glorious in holiness, fearful in praises, doing wonders in
the armies of heaven, and among the inhabitants of the earth.
Moses was put into the cleft of the rock for safety and security;
and so the Lord's living family are sheltered in the cleft of the
Rock, the glorious Person of the dear Redeemer, the Lord
Jesus Christ. Here is their safety and security; here they are safe
in life, safe in the swellings of Jordan, and safe at the judgment
of the great day. What a sweet frame of mind A. M. Toplady
was in, when he penned that solemn and beautiful hymn:—

> Rock of Ages, cleft for me,
> Let me hide myself in Thee!
> Let the water and the blood,
> From thy river side which flow'd,
> Be of sin the double cure,
> Cleanse me from its guilt and pow'r.

This is God's religion. When this is felt in the soul of a sinner it
is the power of God unto salvation. But how blessedly Toplady
speaks of death. I should like, if it were the Lord's will, that
they might be my last words;

Whilst I draw this fleeting breath,
When my eye-strings break in death;
When I soar through tracts unknown,
See Thee on thy judgment-throne;
ROCK of Ages, cleft for me,
Let me hide myself in THEE.

O what a blessed shelter! what a hiding-place! what a refuge from the storm! what a strong tower into which the righteous run and are safe for ever! Well might David say, "The LORD liveth; and blessed be my rock; and let the God of my salvation be exalted."

III.— We notice, in the *third* and last place, *the exaltation of the God of salvation.* "And let the God of my salvation be exalted." The exaltation of the Lord Jesus Christ is a most blessed and precious branch of divine truth, and especially when the child of God is under the same feelings as David was when he penned his beautiful Psalm. The great aim of the apostle Paul, both in preaching and writing was to lay the sinner low in the dust and on the dunghill of self-abasement, and to lift up the Lord Jesus Christ on high — to exalt the sin atoning Lamb, and to crown him Lord of all! I cannot enter into the exaltation of the Lord Jesus Christ more beautifully and strikingly than in the Apostle's language, when he prays for the Ephesian believers that they might know "what is the exceeding greatness of his power toward us who believe, according to the working of his mighty power, which he wrought in Christ, when he raised him from the dead, and set him at his own right hand in the heavenly places, far above all principality, and power, and might, and dominion, and every name which is named, not only in this world, but also in that which is to come." Behold the exaltation of Christ! Here is that very Jesus of Nazareth, who said, "Foxes have holes, and birds of the air have nests; but the Son of man hath not where to lay his head." Here is that same Jesus whom they spat upon, mocked, derided, crowned with a crown of thorns, and at last crucified saying, "it is not fit that he should live." Here is that same Jesus exalted by God the Father, "Far above all principality, and power, and might, and dominion, and every name that is named, not only in this world, but also in that which is to come; and hath put all things under his feet, and given him to be head over all things to the church which is his body the fulness of him that filleth all in all." (Eph. 1. 21-23.) Here is exaltation. He is "King of kings, and Lord of lords!" "The Lord God Omnipotent!" Zion's King, who lives and triumphs evermore!

The Apostle speaks more extensively on the exaltation of Christ, and in order that His exaltation might shine brighter, he contrasts it with His humiliation in this beautiful manner: "Let this mind be in you, which was also in Christ Jesus; who, being in the form of God, thought it not robbery to be equal with God: but made himself of no reputation, and took upon him the form of a servant, and was made in the likeness of men; and being found in fashion as a man, he humbled himself, and became obedient unto death, even the death of the cross." Then comes the exaltation; "Wherefore God also hath highly exalted him, and given him a name which is above every name; that at the name of Jesus every knee should bow, of things in heaven, and things in earth, and things under the earth; and that every tongue should confess that Jesus Christ is Lord to the glory of God the Father." (Phil. 2. 5-11.) The Lord Jesus Christ is exalted far above angels, above the redeemed in glory, and above crowned heads and potentates in the world. He is exalted in nature. He is "King of kings, and Lord of lords;" and as Zion's King he has the preeminence over all things. The Holy Spirit exalts Him in the Bible, where His declarative glory and beauty shines forth in immortal grandeur. "The LORD liveth; and blessed be my rock; and let the God of my salvation be exalted."

Again, wherever the Lord places any of His ambassadors on Zion's wall to blow the silver trumpet of the everlasting gospel, and give it a certain sound, it is the highest ambition of every sent minister of God to exalt Christ in the pulpit — to lift Him high on the pole of the everlasting gospel. As Moses lifted up the serpent in the wilderness, even so must a precious Christ be lifted up and exalted in the hearts and consciences of His own people. And while the preacher is raising up Jesus, there is a feeling of delight kindled in the mind of the believing hearer for he knows the ambassadors of truth can never too much exalt Christ in the glory of His Person, in His covenant engagements, in His atoning blood, and in His law-fulfilling righteousness. The child of God loves to hear Christ lifted up in His finished work, in His resurrection from the dead, in His headship over His church, and in His living advocacy before the throne. He delights to crown Him Lord of all, and that immortal honours should rest on His sacred brow for the great things He has done for his soul. So he says, "The LORD liveth; and blessed be my rock; and let the God of my salvation be exalted."

My friends, do you love to hear Christ lifted up and exalted as your all and in all? If you do you are willing to be made less than nothing and vanity in yourselves. Professors of religion, generally, do not like to be thus humbled; they love to have something to do, in whole or in part, to recommend themselves to God. But the Lord's salvation is not a mixture of grace and works. It is of free and sovereign grace, and received by faith alone, which is the gift of God. It is "not of works, lest any man should boast." The Lord alone be exalted as the Alpha and Omega, the beginning and the ending, the first and the last in the salvation of His people.

Once more with regard to the exaltation of Christ. "And let the God of my salvation be exalted." The Lord Jesus Christ is and must be "the God of salvation," in spite of sin and Satan, death and hell. He must be exalted by the Holy Spirit in the soul of every elect vessel of mercy. An exalted Christ in the Bible without an exalted Christ in the pulpit will not do for the sensible sinner. Christ must be exalted as the all in all in the salvation of His church and people. As sure as the Holy Spirit brings down high and haughty looks; as sure as He abases the proud and lofty, humbles them, and lays them low in the dust of self-abasement, by making them sick of self, stripping them of all their fancied good, and giving them to feel their lost, ruined, and undone state — so sure will this blessed Spirit glorify Jesus by taking of the things of Christ, and shewing them to the heirs of salvation by exalting and lifting Him high in the affections of His people. When the Holy Ghost sheds abroad the Saviour's love in the soul, that soul exalts the Person of the Lord Jesus Christ. Whenever He speaks peace, pardon, joy, and salvation to the conscience, the eternal Spirit has taken of the things of Christ, and shewn them to that conscience. Such a vessel of mercy loves to have Christ exalted in His feelings, and says, "Whom have I in heaven but thee? and there is none upon earth that I desire beside thee." "My beloved is white and ruddy, the chiefest among ten thousand." Christ must be exalted in the hearts and affections of His church and people. These happy moments they have; and the more the Person of Christ is exalted, the more are their feelings melted into gratitude and praise to the God of their salvation. Now David was in this case when he said, "And let the God of my salvation be exalted."

Finally, the God of salvation will be exalted in the morning of the resurrection at the judgment of the great day, when the Lord Jesus Christ will come the second time without sin unto salvation. No longer will He be in the character and capacity of a servant, but in the character and capacity of the Judge of quick and dead. He will come with great power and glory upon the clouds of heaven, with myriads of holy and blessed angels swelling the triumphs of His train. Every eye shall see Him; the trumpet shall sound and the dead be raised; He shall be seated on His great white throne of judgment in solemn majesty and awful power. Assembled worlds shall be arrayed before Him, and ungodly sinners will come forth and stand before that Lord whose name they scorned and whose children they hated and abhorred while upon earth; and they shall hear His awful voice pronouncing to them, "Depart, ye cursed into everlasting fire, prepared for the devil and his angels."

The Lord Jesus Christ will be exalted at the judgment of the great day! He will be the wonder of angels, the terror of devils, and the joy and salvation of His redeemed. He will be exalted far above all principality, and power, and might, and dominion; and at His right hand, in glory and blessedness, will His saints be exalted in eternal honour. "Know ye not, that we shall judge angels?" O with what wonder, glory, and exaltation will the Lord Jesus Christ then appear, surrounded with His saints in glory! "The LORD liveth; and blessed be my rock; and let the God of my salvation be exalted."

God grant, that when the Lord Jesus Christ comes, we may be found among His redeemed, washed from our sins in His precious blood, and clothed in His righteousness! God grant that we may be found sheltered and secure in a precious Christ, the Rock of Ages, the God of our salvation!

2

The River of God

PREACHED AT ZOAR CHAPEL, GREAT ALIE STREET, LONDON,
ON THURSDAY EVENING, APRIL 24, 1845.

"There is a river, the streams whereof shall make glad the city of God." (Psalm 46. 4.)

I shall *first* take notice of the Church of God under the metaphor or title of a "city". In the *second* place I shall speak of the "river" by which this city is made glad. In the *third* place I shall enumerate some of the "streams" that are connected with this river.

1.   The first branch of the subject is *that the church of God is compared to "a city."* Now cities, or at least some of them, are built on an eminence or conspicuous place; and hence they are typical of the Lord's church, which is said to be "a city that is set on a hill," and which "cannot be hid."

Cities generally were walled around, and they had their walls and bulwarks for their safety and defence. So the church of God says, "In that day shall this song be sung in the land of Judah; We have a strong city; salvation will God appoint for walls and bulwarks."

On the walls of these cities there were anciently, and still remain in some places to this day, towers, and in these towers watchmen were placed, both to give an alarm in time of danger, and to fight on the approach of the enemy. So in Zion, the city of the living God, the city of the great King, He has His watch-towers and watchmen; and these watchmen are His ministering servants, who are continually on Zion's walls. The Lord says, "I have set watchmen upon thy walls, O Jerusalem, which shall never hold their peace day nor night; ye that make mention of the LORD, keep not silence. . . till he make Jerusalem a praise in the earth."

We read also in the sacred scriptures, that these watchmen, the Lord's ministering servants, are not merely to stand upon the walls, but they are also to go about the streets and highways of the city to seek the Lord's people. Hence the church says, in the Song of Solomon, when she was seeking her Beloved who had withdrawn himself from her, "The watchmen that go about the city found me." God's ministers go about the city of Zion, and into the abodes of the brethren, to see how they were, and to enquire after their soul's welfare; as Paul and Barnabas did, when they said, "Let us go again and visit our brethren in every city where we have preached the word of the Lord, and see how they do." Thus God's ministers enter into the different stages of the experience of the citizens as in so many of the various streets in Zion, in order to meet their cases, and describe their feelings, by pointing out who they are, and where they are.

Again, cities have their chief and principal men. So, in reference to Zion, "the city of the living God," it is called "the city of the great King," King Jesus. "I have set my king upon my holy hill of Zion," the church of God. Jesus Christ is King in Zion; and the church is His city. His habitation, and His dwelling-place. He says, "This is my rest for ever; here will I dwell; for I have desired it." The inhabitants of this city of Zion are heaven-born and Spirit-taught souls, for they are all born in the city. But in reference to citizens literally, they are not all free-born, for some have to purchase their freedom. In the case of Paul when they were about scourging him, he being a Roman and uncondemned, the chief captain said to him, "With a great sum obtained I this freedom. And Paul said, But I was free-born." So the inhabitants of spiritual Zion, the people of God, are all free born citizens. When the Lord makes up the number of His people, it shall be said, "this and that man was born in her." Jerusalem is said to "travail in birth," and "to bring forth;" and she is said also to be "the mother of us all."

In Jerusalem God clothes His word with almighty power and sinners are converted; here they are born again of the Spirit and brought into newness of life; and, as Peter says, are "begotten again unto a lively hope by the resurrection of Jesus Christ from the dead." So that all real spiritual citizens of Zion, are heaven-born and Spirit-taught souls, and constitute the church and "city of the living God."

Time would fail me were I to attempt to point out the marks and evidences of these spiritual citizens and heaven-born souls. We find the King of the city says, "Except a man be born again, he cannot see the kingdom of God;" and "Except ye be converted, and become as little children, ye shall not enter into the kingdom of heaven." Every true citizen, therefore, must be a converted character and will be brought to feel himself as a little child. But in what sense of the word does the true citizen of Zion become as a little child? I would direct your attention to the new-born babe, described by the prophet Ezekiel, who was cast out into the open field in a state of destitution and wretchedness. That was a little child in very indigent and pitiable circumstances, emblematical of a heaven born soul. How weak, how helpless that child was! — but yet no more weak or helpless than the heaven-born soul is made to see and feel himself to be. That little child could do nothing at all for itself: it could not wash, feed, dress, nor clothe itself; neither could it protect or defend itself; it must have everything done for it. So heaven-born souls, regenerate by the Holy Spirit, feel that they can do nothing for themselves, but add sin to sin; they must have everything done for them. And blessed be the name of the King, He has done it all. As the Captain of our salvation, He has finished redemption's work. There is everything in the Monarch of this city that its citizens stand in need of. Glorious things are spoken of the city, and of the King of the city, and of the treasures and supplies that He has laid up to meet the wants and necessities of the citizens. It is out of His fulness that they are said to receive, "and grace for grace." Under the same metaphor of a babe, Peter speaks of every regenerate soul; "as new-born babes desire the sincere milk of the word." These heaven born souls, who are begotten of God in this spiritual city of Zion, have an earnest and hearty desire for God's truth and its ministration, that through it they "may grow thereby." Real citizens, who are born again of God, bear these marks and evidences, and many more also.

Now, in reference to the government of the city, there is the monarch, and there are the laws and regulations of the city. In an English city you have your Lord Mayor, aldermen, and common councilmen; and these sit and deliberate on all the affairs of the city. So, as it regards Zion, "the city of the great King;" He governs it, for "the government is upon his shoulders." It is said, "out of Zion shall go forth the law, and the word of the LORD from Jerusalem." But for the ordering of the city, and the execution of the laws of Zion's King, He raises up His ministering servants, who are not only to preach the glad tidings of salvation, but to bear rule in the church of God in the name of the King. "Let the elders that rule well be counted worthy of double honour, especially they who labour in the word and doctrine." There is to be no lordship nor authority in the city; this belongs only to the King, the Lord Jesus Christ. "Ye call me Lord and Master; and ye say well, for so I am." But for the order and regulation of the city, the officers of the church of God are to see that the laws and statutes of King Jesus are properly attended to; and the word of the Lord has given directions to accomplish this end. "All scripture is given by inspiration of God, and is profitable for doctrine, for reproof, for correction, for instruction in righteousness; that the man of God may be perfect, throughly furnished unto all good works." So then, this city of the King of kings, and its inhabitants, spiritual men and spiritual women, are built upon Christ, the Rock of Ages. In this blessed city, they are swayed and governed by Jesus Christ, and here He rules over them by a holy sceptre, even the sceptre of His love and righteousness.

II. — Let us now come to *"the river."* "There is a river, the streams whereof make glad the city of God."

1.   *This blessed river is the love of the triune God, the everlasting electing love of Jehovah.* We read of it in the sacred scriptures as "a pure river of water of life. . . proceeding out of the throne of God and of the Lamb." It runs all through time and will flow on in an unfathomable ocean throughout a never-ending eternity. Wherever there is an elect vessel of mercy, covenant love will be sure to find him out; it will discover him by regenerating grace in the appointed time, and arrest him in his conscience. One of our hymns expresses it—

"Almighty love arrest that man!"

The Lord loved Saul of Tarsus; and as the effect of that love, He arrested him in his conscience. So, in a similar way, He will arrest every one whom He has loved from eternity, and bring him to His blessed feet; He will begin in him the good work of grace, carry it on, and land him at last safe in immortal glory. Thus God's covenant love, His everlasting electing love, is a river springing up into eternal life. It began in Jehovah's eternal counsel and purpose; it runs on through time, and flows into eternity, making glad the objects of His love and choice. This is the river, God's electing love, "the streams whereof make glad the city of God."

The Prophet Ezekiel, speaking on the subject of this river in its manifestations to the children of men, describes it in its first flowings forth as only "up to the ankles." Now, might not this represent the patriarchal dispensation? for in that dark period, very little of the glory of God, or the covenant love of Jehovah, were discoverable. Then, in the next place, he speaks of it as being "up to the knees." Might not this represent the Mosaic dispensation, in which there was a multitude of rites and ceremonies, and all pointing to the Lord Jesus Christ? And when he goes on to speak of the river as still rising higher, and coming to "the loins" — might not that represent the prophetic age, in which holy men spake more explicitly of the breakings forth of God's covenant love and mercy? At length we find the river so increased, that it is represented as "waters to swim in, a river that could not be passed over." O, God's covenant love bursting forth in the incarnation of the Lord Jesus Christ, is a river so broad that there is no swimming over it! "God so loved the world, that he gave his only begotten Son, that whosoever believeth in him should not perish, but have everlasting life." And the manifestation of this blessed love by the Holy Spirit to the souls of His people — this also is a river that never, never can be crossed: yea, God's covenant love is a boundless, bottomless sea to the inhabitants of this city.

Paul says, in writing to the Ephesians, "For this cause I bow my knees unto the Father of our Lord Jesus Christ, of whom the whole family in heaven and earth is named; that he would grant you, according to the riches of his glory, to be strengthened with might by his Spirit in the inner man; that Christ may dwell in your hearts by faith; that ye, being rooted and grounded in love, may be able to comprehend with all saints what is the breadth, and length, and depth, and height;

and to know the love of Christ." Yet, the Apostle Paul knew that neither the breadth, length, depth, nor height of the love of God could be described, for he says, it "passeth knowledge." William Huntington's sermon entitled, 'The Dimensions of Eternal Love' is one of the best discourses on God's covenant love I have ever seen.

2. *The Lord Jesus Christ* is particularly spoken of as a river. We cannot well separate God's covenant love from our Lord Jesus Christ, nor our Lord Jesus Christ from God's covenant love; for His glorious Person is the blessed channel through which the love of Jehovah's heart, and the love of His own heart, flow towards guilty sinners. The prophet Isaiah is directed to speak of it in this beautifully figurative language: "And a man shall be as an hiding place from the wind, and a covert from the tempest; as rivers of water in a dry place, as the shadow of a great rock in a weary land." Our Lord Jesus Christ is this "river of water in a dry place."

Is not the church of God in herself a dry and barren land, without this blessed river? I hope and trust I am one of the citizens; but what hardness, dryness, and barrenness do I often feel in my soul! How I need this blessed river, the Lord Jesus Christ, to flow into my soul, to water it and make it fruitful in every good word and work! The same prophet, speaking of Christ, says, "But there the glorious LORD will be unto us as a place of broad rivers and streams;" so that our Lord Jesus Christ is a place of broad rivers and streams to His citizens. We have this illustration both in the type and in the antitype itself. The children of Israel travelling through the wilderness, were typical of the Lord's family travelling through this world. They were in a desert land, and wanted water to drink; Moses smote the rock at Horeb, and there flowed from the smitten rock a river, a fountain, a stream of water; and wherever God's Israel went in all their turnings and windings, this river flowed after them, to supply their wants and necessities. The apostle Paul, writing to the church at Corinth, mentions this very circumstance. He says, "They all drank of that spiritual rock that followed them, and that rock was Christ." The water flowing from that rock is typical of the stream that flows from the Redeemer, and supplies the wants and necessities of His people in this time state. And do we not need the Lord's love, and His precious atoning blood, to follow us like a river that so we may drink of the brook by the way, and obtain joy and peace to our precious souls? What a mercy it is to be enabled to bathe in this fountain of the love and blood of a dear Redeemer! The citizens stand in need of this river. "When the poor and needy seek water, and there is none, and their tongue faileth them for thirst, I the LORD will hear them, I the God of Israel will not forsake them. I will open rivers in high places, and fountains in the midst of the valleys; I will make the wilderness a pool of water, and the dry land springs of water." The Lord Jesus Christ, then, is a glorious river to the spiritual inhabitants of this city.

3. *The Holy Ghost and His divine influences,* are compared in the scriptures to a river. If we turn our attention to John 7. 37, 38, we shall see it there blessedly set forth. "In the last day, that great day of the feast, Jesus stood and cried, saying, If any man thirst, let him come unto me and drink. He that believeth in me, as the scripture hath said, out of his belly shall flow rivers of living water." Wherever the Holy Spirit dwells in the soul of a sinner, He dwells in him as a river, as a fountain. Hence our Lord said to the woman of Samaria whom He met at Jacob's well, "Whosoever drinketh of this water shall thirst again; but whosoever drinketh the water that I shall give him, shall never thirst; but the water that I shall give him shall be in him a well of water springing up into everlasting life." So "there is a river, the streams whereof make glad the city of God."

It is a great mercy for a village to be well watered; but it is a greater mercy for a town, and especially for a large city, to have plenty of water. London could never have grown to what it is, in point of magnitude, were it not for the river that flows through it, and the bountiful springs of water that surround it. Zion, "the city of the living God," is watered with the river of the Holy Spirit of God. "There is a river, the streams whereof make glad the city of our God."

III. — Having made these remarks upon the river itself, we now take notice of *"the streams* which make glad the city of God." There are streams connected with this river that gladden the hearts of the spiritual citizens of Zion. What are these streams?

1. In the first place — *the invitations of the gospel* are one of the streams of this river, which, under the influence of the

Holy Ghost, flow into and gladden the heart of the citizens. Is a spiritual citizen sighing, faint and discouraged because of the troubles of the way? Is his mind cast down and oppressed, so that he can scarcely crawl along? I am sometimes so weary, undone, and oppressed in my feelings, that I know not what to do. Well, the King of the city stoops to the citizens, and He says, "Come unto me, all ye that labour, and are heavy laden, and I will give you rest." Let the Holy Spirit cause this sweet stream to flow into the soul of the citizen, and it will draw him along with it to the dear Redeemer. He will sit down at the feet of his Lord, as beneath the shadow of a great rock in a weary land, and find rest to his soul. It is as this stream brings us near to a precious Christ, that we can cast our burden upon Him, and He sustains us; as Peter says, "Casting all your care upon him, for he careth for you." And thus, "All that the Father giveth me," says the King of the city, "shall come unto me." So this sweet stream, flowing from the blessed river, lays hold of a sinner, and brings him to Jesus.

Come, then, poor, weary, heavy-laden soul; however many your sins are, however hard your heart is, however filthy and depraved you may see yourself to be, the King of the city says, "Him that cometh unto me, I will in no wise cast out." He never casts out any that come to Him, unless they come with a price in their hands; then He will have nothing at all to do with them, but will send them empty away. Bless His precious name — and it does my soul good as I talk to you about it — He will have nothing to do with any but beggars and insolvents! He says to such, "Come ye, buy, and eat; yea, come, buy wine and milk without money and without price." O this is glorious to a sinner who knows he has nothing to bring, and feels himself utterly worthless. The sweet stream of gospel invitations thus gladdens the heart of the citizen of Zion. He feels himself thirsty, faint, and drooping, and he wants reviving and cheering. He wants a sweet taste of the water of life, a drop of the good old wine of the kingdom, and to drink of the stream that flows from this river, and that speaks thus, "Ho every one that thirsteth, come ye to the waters, and he that hath no money; come ye, buy and eat; yea, come, buy wine and milk, without money and without price." O blessed invitation! May the Holy Spirit cause it to flow into the hearts of the citizens of Zion! May they be encouraged to come to "the fountain of living waters"! "The Spirit and the bride say, Come. And let him that heareth say, Come. And let him that is athirst come. And whosoever will, let him take the water of life freely."

'O,' say some, 'but that does not fit you; you are a pre-destinarian. Here is a universal invitation, a stream flowing to everybody.' But, I see God's election in that text. 'You must have eagle eyes to see election there.' Well, let us try it by God's rule. "Whosoever will, let him come." Who is the man that will come? The man in a state of nature? O no. The Lord Himself says, "Ye will not come unto me, that ye might have life." Man's will is opposed to coming; my will was opposed to coming once; but the Psalmist says, "Thy people shall be willing in the day of thy power." God makes His people willing; and the gospel invitation is, "Whosoever will, let him come." But what are these invitations to us, if we are not willing? So, the invitations of the gospel are one of the streams of this river, which make glad the hearts of the citizens of Zion.

2. Another stream that flows from this river and makes glad the heart of the spiritual citizen, is *pardoning love and mercy*. This is a very sweet and gladdening stream; but it is neither sweet nor gladdening to those who do not feel themselves guilty and condemned. If you and I were talking of pardoning and forgiving a person, and that person were not conscious he had offended us, instead of cheering his heart, it would offend him: he would say, 'I do not want your mercy and pardon; I have not trespassed upon you, be it known to you.' But pardon and forgiveness are sweet to the guilty and condemned citizens of Zion, who have had God's law carried into their conscience. If the law has taken hold of the citizen by the throat, and said, "Pay me that thou owest;" if he has been weighed in the balances of the sanctuary, and found wanting; if he has been tried in the court of conscience he has been found guilty, both as it respects his outward actions and his inward intentions; for the Holy Spirit "is a discerner of the thoughts and intents of the heart." Many professors of religion think they are all right, so long as they can keep the outside of the cup and platter clean; and men think that such persons are very good and pious creatures, as long as this is the case; but all the while their hearts are guilty before God. But when the citizen of Zion feels that he is guilty within and without, that he is a condemned and miserable wretch, then pardoning mercy is sweet to him. There is not a real spiritual citizen of Zion, who

is not crying and groaning in his mind because of his sins, and pleading for mercy and grace through Christ; for he makes Christ his only plea.

We read in 1 Kings 20, 31 of the servants of Benhadad saying to him after he had been overcome in battle, and fled away for safety, "Behold now, we have heard that the kings of the house of Israel are merciful kings; let us, I pray thee, put sackcloth on our loins, and ropes upon our heads, and go out to the king of Israel: peradventure he will save thy life." Now God brings every citizen of Zion before Him in his feelings, with sackcloth on his body and a rope round his neck, to fall down before His blessed Majesty, saying, 'O Lord, if Thou shouldest send me to hell, Thou wouldst be a just King! I deserve no favour at Thy hands; for I am a vile, guilty, and polluted criminal.' Therefore he cries with the publican, "God be merciful to me a sinner!" And was there not mercy in the heart of the king of Israel towards Benhadad when the servants came thus before him? Yes; for he took him up in his chariot, and caused him to ride with him. And is not the King of the city of Zion a merciful king? Does He not manifest His love to sinners? We see it in the case of Mary Magdalene. She came to the feet of Jesus with a broken and contrite heart; she was a mourner over sin, and wept before Him. But the Lord spake to her, and said, "Woman, thy sins which are many, are all forgiven thee." The streams of pardon flowed into her soul like a river, and caused a flood of tears to trickle down her cheeks. So with many others recorded in the scriptures this blessed stream of gospel mercy flowed into their hearts, giving them joy and peace. The prophet Micah felt it; for he said, "Who is a God like unto thee, that pardoneth iniquity, and passeth by the transgressions of the remnant of his heritage? he retaineth not his anger for ever, because he delighteth in mercy." Is there a sweeter word than this in all the Bible? Come, poor guilty sinner, you have to do with a God that "delighteth in mercy;" your cry has gone up to Him; and the streams of His mercy flow towards you. He says, "I will have mercy upon whom I will have mercy; and I will have compassion upon whom I will have compassion."

There is a declaration on this point which has flowed into my soul as a stream, and that has helped me on for many a year. I do not know what I could have done without it. The covenant God, speaking of the greatness of His mercy, says, "Behold, the days come, saith the LORD, that I will make a new covenant with the house of Israel, and with the house of Judah; . . . I will put my laws into their minds, and I will write them in their hearts: and I will be to them a God, and they shall be to me a people. For I will be merciful to their unrighteousness, and their sins and their iniquities will I remember no more." This is an exceeding great and precious promise of covenant mercy! It brings joy into my soul that I have to do with a God that says, "I will be merciful:" so that neither my sins, nor the devil, nor all the opposition that I feel from within or without can ever turn away His love from my soul. This fills my heart with gladness, and makes it shout for joy. It was the streams of this river, that flowed into the heart of the poor dying thief, and gladdened his heart; and this same stream flows into the souls of all true citizens, making glad their hearts, and will continue to do so till every vessel of mercy is landed safe in immortal glory.

There may be some citizens who are saying, 'I wish these streams of mercy would flow into my soul; I have been long beseeching the Lord to speak peace and pardon to my conscience, by saying, "Son, or daughter, go in peace." Sometimes I have thought the streams of the Lord's pardoning mercy were coming at last, but I am now all in doubt about it, and fear that they will never be mine.' Well, well, poor soul, be not dismayed; wait on the Lord; "Be of good courage, and he shall strengthen your heart, all ye that hope in the Lord." "The vision is for an appointed time, but at the end it shall speak, and not lie: though it tarry, wait for it: because it will surely come, it will not tarry." Christ has shed His blood for the sins of His people; and the Holy Ghost will apply that precious blood to the consciences of the citizens, that they may feel its efficacy in purging away their guilt. By this sacred stream they are made as holy as Christ is holy, and as pure as He is pure. Paul says, "Christ also loved the church, and gave himself for it; that he might sanctify and cleanse it with the washing of water by the word, that he might present it to himself a glorious church, not having spot, or wrinkle, or any such thing." The stream of pardoning love and mercy is a blessed stream that flows from this river to make glad the citizens of Zion.

3.   *The promises of the gospel* are another blessed stream that flows from this river to make glad the heart of the spiritual

citizens. Peter says there "are given unto us exceeding great and precious promises." What makes them so exceedingly great and precious, and comforting to the hearts of God's people is, that they are unconditional! 'But,' say you, 'how are God's promises unconditional? They are unconditional to us because they do not depend for their fulfilment upon any obedience of ours; if they did, all their preciousness and sweetness would be gone. I cannot come before the Lord, and plead for any of His blessings on the ground of my own obedience or worthiness. Now can you, my friends? 'O no,' you say, 'this is not the way.' All the promises of God in the Lord Jesus are all "yea and amen," that is, sure and certain, and "to the glory of God by us." This constitutes a great part of the sweetness of the promises.

Do you not see how this meets the case of the Lord's people? The citizen comes before the King, and pleads with him, telling him his tale of woe. I am pleased with the tale of woe, and shall be as long as I live; and if you have not the same tale to tell the King, I very much doubt your citizenship, for every citizen is brought into the same feelings. He says, "O Lord, I am not worthy of the least of these thy mercies!" 'Well,' say you, 'I do feel this; it is the language of my heart and soul, and fits me well.' So the prayer of the spiritual citizen is,'Heavenly Father, I cannot do without Thy blessings; I ask and plead for them in the name of Jesus, for He has said, "Whatsoever ye shall ask the Father in my name, he will give it you." Do then look upon me, heavenly Father, in the name of Jesus; look upon me in the face of thine Anointed. O Lord, look down upon me, and help and bless me!' As the promise is brought home to your heart, under the bedewing influences of the Holy Spirit, the Lord will help and support you. He will uphold the heart of the righteous; He will strengthen them in the inner man; for He says, "I will never leave thee, nor forsake thee." He will go with them through the floods and the flames; be with them in the fiery furnace, and surely do them good.

If you have sat under the best preacher, you will want to sit under him again. 'Well,' say you, 'but who do you call the best preacher?' I will tell you, fearless of contradiction, who the best preacher is — it is the Holy Ghost! If you have been brought to the feet of Jesus; if the promises have been applied to your heart, and you have felt their sweetness and preciousness, you have been under the teachings of the Holy

Spirit, and you know something of the streams of consolation and joy that make glad the heart of the citizens, and which flow from the righteousness and faithfulness of a covenant-keeping God.

One particular season in my experience comes into my mind. It was before I had entered the ministry, and some time after I had enjoyed peace and pardon, through an application of the precious blood of the cross. I was brought into what is called the 'weaning time,' as it is said, "Whom shall he teach knowledge? and whom shall he make to understand doctrine? them that are weaned from the milk, and drawn from the breasts." I was now in great bondage, and sadly tempted to believe that all my religion was only a delusion, that I was only a stony-ground hearer, and that the seed of the word had been choked by the cares of the world. How my soul sunk within me because I had joined the church, and had gone among the Lord's people, telling them what He had done for my soul! In this dark season, when the temptations of the Devil prevailed against me, I said, 'I wished I had never joined the church, for I was sure I should soon fall, and bring a disgrace upon the cause.' Weeks and months passed by, during which my soul remained in a dark and stupid state; yet the Lord was at work upon me all the while. I felt such groanings and sighings to the Lord day and night: and at every opportunity I was found at the throne of grace beseeching Him to appear for me. I think I now see the place, it is in the eye of my mind while I am now talking with you. But when I was upon my knees sighing and breathing out the desires of my soul to the Lord, these words were dropped into my heart by the Holy Ghost. "The eyes of the LORD are upon the righteous, and his ear is open to their cry." From that sweet text, I was led from one portion to another; and the Holy Spirit preached to my soul a sermon at that time which I shall never forget. Afterwards I walked to and fro in the fields under these blessed bedewings, and felt such streams of joy and gladness in my heart that I never felt before.

It is as the streams of this river flow into the heart, through the sweet influences of the Holy Spirit, that the citizens of the city of God, the Church of the living God, are made glad. May the Lord cause these streams of mercy to flow into our souls more powerfully, that our hearts may be made glad, and that we may rejoice and triumph in the Lord alone.

3

The Ministry

PREACHED AT FORD STREET CHAPEL, COVENTRY
ON WEDNESDAY EVENING, MARCH 27TH, 1867.

"And they went forth, and preached every where, the Lord working with them, and confirming the word with signs following. Amen." (Mark 16. 20).

Beloved, holy men were inspired and directed by the Lord the Holy Spirit to give us a full and particular account of the crucifixion of our Lord Jesus Christ on Calvary's cross, where He died for our sins and where He was delivered for our offences, and raised again for our justification. They spoke particularly, not only of His crucifixion, but of His death, His burial, and His resurrection from the dead, of His being the plague of death, and the destruction of the grave. We have a highly interesting account by the evangelists of His appearing after His resurrection to the women, to the two disciples going to Emmaus, and to the disciples assembled in an upper room.

As the great Head of the Church the Lord Jesus Christ gave to His ministers, whom He had appointed preachers of His gospel and founders of the gospel dispensation, their commission; that they were to stay at Jerusalem till they were endued with power from on high, till the day of Pentecost; that repentance and remission of sins should be preached in His name among all nations, beginning at Jerusalem; that they were to preach the gospel to every creature; and that "He that believeth and is baptized shall be saved, but he that believeth not shall be damned." The Lord gave them their commission on the Mount of Olives, where we find the disciples and apostles assembled before Him. In giving the charge He lifts up His arms, blessing them, and saying, "All power is given unto me in heaven and in earth." And in the very act of blessing them, He ascended up on high, led captivity captive, and entered the pearly gates of the celestial city. "He led captivity captive, and gave gifts unto men." "He gave some, apostles; and some prophets; and some evangelists; and some, pastors and teachers; for the perfecting of the saints for the work of the ministry."

Now in our text it is said of the apostles that they went forth according to the direction they had received from Him. "They went forth, and preached everywhere, the Lord working with them, and confirming the word with signs following."

I would illustrate the text in the following order:

I. *The characters* that are said to go forth;
II. Their going forth everywhere;
III. The Lord working with them;
IV. *Confirming* the word with *signs following.*

I. The *characters* who are said to go forth. *"They* went forth." These were His ministering servants. The Lord has established ·in His church a standing ministry of His word to the end of time. This is embodied in that precious promise He made to His ministering servants: "Lo, I am with you alway, even to the end of the world." God's ministers, like the high priests under the law, by reason of death were not suffered to continue, only so long as·to finish the work He had appointed for them. He with whom is the residue of the Spirit, raises up, fits, qualifies, and sends forth others to fill their places; as it is written: "How shall they hear without a preacher? And how shall they preach except they be sent?" Our Lord has established a standing ministry as long as His church remains in a militant state, not only for the gathering in of the number of His elect that are scattered abroad, but for the comforting, edifying, and building up of His people. It is His prerogative to make choice of them. He has promised a succession of them. He has promised to give His church pastors after His own heart, that shall feed them with knowledge and understanding. (Jer. 3.

15.) We look to Him for the fulfilment of this prayer: That the Lord would raise up and send forth more labourers into His vineyard; men to go forth everywhere to preach the glorious gospel of a free-grace salvation. We are looking up, then, to the great Head of the church for a succession of faithful, God-fearing, experimental ministers, thrust forth to labour among His people in word and doctrine.

We would here observe that no man can be said to be called, anointed, and sent out to go and preach the gospel, unless He is born again of the Spirit of God, and made a new creature in Christ Jesus. How can a man preach Christ Jesus for the comfort and edification of the family of God who has never felt the comfort and consolation of the gospel in his own soul? The ministers of the Lord Jesus Christ, having felt that comfort, are able to comfort them which are in any trouble by the comfort wherewith they are themselves comforted of God. Hence the command of God by the mouth of the prophet Isaiah: "Comfort ye, comfort ye my people, saith your God. Speak ye comfortably to Jerusalem, and cry unto her, that her warfare is accomplished, that her iniquity is pardoned; for she hath received of the LORD'S hand double for all her sins." (40. 1.)

Be it also observed that *not all* those to whom God is gracious, not all who are born of God and taught by His Spirit, are called and sent forth to preach the gospel. Even those good and gracious men who, like the apostles, had been witnesses of the sufferings and death of Christ, were not to go forth till they were endued with power from on high. When the day of Pentecost was come, they received that anointing which fitted and qualified them for the work. They were then sent forth; and they went forth preaching the word, the Lord working with them.

Here we would contrast two things. First, — The child of God is concerned to prove that he really does belong to the family of God; that he is one of His chosen, predestinated family. How, then, is he to prove this? By his being effectually called by grace. How many of God's children, in reference to their personal interest in the finished salvation of Jesus Christ, spend much time in examination of themselves by prayer, supplication, and attending the means of grace, that they may have the Spirit's witness, and the assurance of the Holy Ghost that they belong to the Lord. What a mercy it is to know our election of God! This can only be known by effectual calling.

Second, — To draw the contrast between calling and going forth to preach the gospel take notice that every man called of God to go forth to preach the gospel has *an especial call* to the work. Paul says, when referring to the subject, "To me, who am less than the least of all saints, *is this grace given,* that I should preach among the Gentiles the unsearchable riches of Christ." The apostle had grace in Christ before the world was, as he was one in the covenant made with Christ, and was given to Christ. He means here that in time this grace was especially made manifest, when Christ revealed Himself to him. But he had also *special grace* given to him, to qualify, fit, anoint, and send him forth to preach the gospel.

"And they went forth, and preached everywhere, the Lord working with them, and confirming the word with signs following." Many of God's ministers spend as much time, if not more, in earnest prayer, supplication, and wrestling with the Lord in reference to their call to the work of the ministry, than they do in reference to their call by grace. The minister in the pulpit before you, who has stood on Zion's walls more than fifty years, had more exercises and wrestlings with the Lord in reference to his being sent of God to preach the gospel than he had with respect to his effectual call by grace.

It is needful that a man who goes forth in his Master's service should have his master's commission, should know it, and should have His sanction and divine approbation. The apostles knew this, and they went forth. None could fit and qualify them but the great Head of the church, for that situation which the Lord had appointed for them. In accomplishing this, the Lord makes use of instruments. He lays the work of the ministry on the minds of such as He designs to send forth. Therefore with such there is a solemn groaning, sighing, and crying, a feeling of their unworthiness and insufficiency. They labour and do all they can to remove the impression. That God, however, who has begun the work, still stirs them up. They have no rest. His truth in them is like the word in Jeremiah, "as a burning fire shut up in my bones and I was weary with forbearing, and I could not stay." Thus, being a child of God, he has no rest. The Lord lays it on the hearts of the brethren and sisters, who pray for him, and encourage him. He that spoke to the church at Antioch, as we read: "The Holy Ghost said, Separate me Barnabas and Saul for the work whereunto I have called them," lays it on the minds of the brethren that the Lord has designed them for the work of the ministry.

The Lord also leads those he designs for public usefulness more deeply and solemnly into gospel truth. When such are called upon to engage in prayer in public, the people find a savour, dew, and unction attending their prayers. When they enter into conversation, or give their thoughts on a portion of God's Word for godly edification, there is a savour and power that enters the minds of God's people, draws their affections, and knits their hearts toward them. This so draws their minds forth that they encourage them and bring them forward. Thus, sanctioned by the Lord, and encouraged by the church, they go forth and preach everywhere, the Lord working with them.

Now if any man thrusts himself forward, you may rest satisfied he will not be a blessing to the church of God. We read of Moses and of Gideon; how backward they were, and what excuse they made. So it is with others of the Lord's family. Their language is, "Send by the hand of him whom thou wilt send; but do not send *me.*" They are fully impressed with the importance of the work, standing up before the living God to speak to the never dying souls of their fellow creatures. They come trembling; and the brethren and sisters, seeing this, pray for and encourage them; and they have the testimony of the Lord that their labour is not in vain. These "go forth" to preach the gospel, having the sanction of the great Head of the church and approbation of the brethren, who pour out their prayers and supplications to God. The Lord works with them.

II. The second branch of my subject is, "They went forth and preached everywhere." What did they preach? *Not themselves.* No, not themselves, but Christ Jesus the Lord. Why did they preach Him? Because they were specially anointed to preach Him. And this was not the only reason. They had enjoyed the Lord in their own souls as their Saviour and their Redeemer, whose love had been sweetly shed abroad in their heart. They had been led to see that His righteousness alone would justify them. They had seen by faith His atoning sacrifice, to deliver them from guilt and condemnation, and His efficacious blood to cleanse from every stain. This has been made so precious and comforting to their souls, the Lord's power and ability to save so much felt, so powerfully impressed upon their hearts, that a necessity was laid upon them to preach. "Woe is unto me," said the apostle, "if I preach not the gospel."

"They went forth and preached everywhere." We see the example in reference to Saul of Tarsus. When called by grace, he preached in the synagogue that Jesus is the Son of God, proving it from the records of heaven. Peter was anointed to preach the gospel; he went everywhere preaching the Word. When mentioning the circumstance of the healing of the lame man who sat at the gate called Beautiful asking for alms, and when before the rulers in the face of the greatest opposition, when asked by what power or name they had done this, Peter replied, "Be it known unto you, and to all the people, that by the name of Jesus Christ of Nazareth, whom ye crucified, whom God raised from the dead, even by him, doth this man stand here before you whole. . . Neither is there salvation in any other; for there is none other name under heaven given among men, whereby we must be saved." By the precious blood alone of Jesus can we be saved from our sins and all the damning consequences of them. They preached that Christ was exalted to give repentance to Israel, and remission of sins.

When the disciples were scattered abroad on account of the persecution that arose, Stephen went out and preached Jesus. Wherever he went, he preached a precious Christ in the heart, the hope of glory. "They ceased not to teach and to preach," to exalt the Redeemer in His everlasting gospel; the Lord by them confirming the word in the souls of the people.

Again, when Philip went down to Samaria, he preached Jesus Christ to the Ethiopian eunuch in his chariot. "He opened his mouth and preached unto him Jesus." They "went forth;" and wherever they went they exalted the Lamb of God, the sin-atoning Lamb. They preached the Redeemer as the alone name whereby sinners can be saved; so that precious souls were comforted and satisfied. The Lord himself says, "Look unto me and be ye saved, all the ends of the earth; for I am God, and there is none else."

The ministers of Christ are never so happy as when they are under the anointing of the Holy Spirit, exalting the Lamb of God, encouraging law-condemned sinners to look by faith to Jesus, to believe on Him, and encouraging souls to commit their cause into His hands. There is no safety or security anywhere but in Jesus. They went everywhere, and not only preached Jesus, but preached Him as the only name whereby sinners could be saved; the only way whereby God can be just, and the justifier of sinners. "I am," says Jesus, "the way, the truth, and the life." No man can come to the Father or to heaven but by and through the rent veil of the Redeemer's flesh. This is the only way by which we draw nigh to God.

The minister who preaches Jesus exalts Him as the living way. He takes the stones out of the way, and lifts up the Lord as an ensign to the people, as the only way by which we draw nigh to God, the only way whereby we can be saved from sin, the only way of worship the Lord owns and blesses, and the only way to the realms of everlasting bliss and blessedness. There is no other way but this. The apostles were valiant for this truth. They maintained at all hazards that there was no way of access to the Father but by Jesus Christ. They went forth and preached this everywhere. The apostle is very explicit about this, He says, "For I determined to know nothing among you save Jesus Christ, and him crucified." He was determined to bring forward no other. He tells us this is the only foundation: "Other foundation can no man lay than that is laid, which is Jesus Christ," and he instructs others to build upon Jesus Christ, who is the sure foundation stone.

"They went forth, preaching everywhere," razing all false foundations, removing all false refuges of lies, and preaching Jesus Christ as the only ground and foundation of a sinner's hope. God's ministers, going forth preaching Jesus, can never lay the sinner too low, nor ever lift the Redeemer too high. This is sound speech that cannot be condemned: "Lord, lay me in the dust of self-abasement, poor, sinful, filthy and worthless. But when Jesus is preached, let Him be exalted and lifted up in His glorious Person as the incarnate God. Let Him be exalted in his covenant engagements, on the ground of His obedience, as the Lamb for His great atoning sacrifice, in the power of His resurrection, in the glory of His ascension to heaven, and in His prevailing intercession for the souls of His living family."

When Jesus is thus preached by His ministers, the Lord works by them. The word applied by the Holy Spirit produces feelings in the soul similar to this: "Whom have I in heaven but thee? And there is none upon earth that I desire beside thee." Have you ever felt thus? "He is the chiefest among ten thousand, and the altogether lovely." "Bring forth the royal diadem, and crown him Lord of all!" This is the language of the soul that goes forth preaching Christ. Paul says, "Some indeed preach Christ of envy and strife; and some also of good will: The one preach Christ of contention, not sincerely, supposing to add affliction to my bonds; but the other of love, knowing I am set for the defence of the gospel. What then? Notwithstanding, every way, whether in pretence, or in truth, Christ is preached; and I therein do rejoice, and will rejoice." What benefit or profit is there to a living soul if a minister comes preaching, if Christ is not the Alpha and Omega, the beginning and the end of our preaching? However eloquent the language and beautiful the style, God's family is not comforted; the church is not edified.

III. The third part of the subject is *"the Lord working"* by or with them. If the Lord does not work by His ministers, their preaching will be in vain.

Before I come to dwell particularly on this point, it will be needful to make an observation lest the language of the apostle Paul might be taken in a wrong sense. I will put two passages together. "The Lord working with them." Paul says, "We then, as workers together with God, beseech you that ye receive not the grace of God in vain." From this portion some would tell us that we are co-workers with God in salvation matters. This will not do as it respects the work of salvation. Christ finished that work upon the cross. His own arm brought salvation, and of the people there were none with Him. Salvation belongeth to the Lord. The Lord is the Saviour of souls. He provided the way for us to heaven, and saved us from the wrath to come. What, then, is intended by "everywhere they went forth, the Lord working with them," and "they working with the Lord"? *Not* that we are co-workers with God in salvation matters. In the salvation of the soul the Lord Jesus is all in all. How, then, does the Lord work with them, and they work with the Lord?

"The Lord working with them." God's ministers, the Lord's servants, do not want to move in the ministry of the word without consulting their blessed Lord and Master. They want His divine approbation, His direction, His instruction; and as He works with them, so they work in their preaching. Say you, "How so?" A sent minister of God, whether itinerating or settled over a people, enters into his closet, not to get his sermon from books. The apostles, in speaking upon this, said, "It is not reason that we should leave the word of God, and serve tables; but we will give ourselves continually to prayer and the ministry of the word."

The speaker before you has fallen down before his Lord and master many times for a portion of the Word to be impressed on his mind. He has given himself to prayer for a portion of God's Word to be laid upon his mind, and that the Holy Spirit would bring some particular portion with savour and unction to his heart. Thus, then, the Lord, working with him, takes forth His heavenly treasure, puts it into the earthen vessel, and brings forth desires out of the man's heart Godward, for the comfort and edifying of the household of faith. He, under the influence of the Holy Spirit, is led to bring forth those precious truths which he feels savoury in his own soul, and which he has experienced. Thus he commends the glorious truths of the gospel. "The husbandman that laboureth must be first partaker of the fruits." The time comes for the labourer to go forth from his closet. A door is open, he ascends the pulpit, trembling at the idea of standing up before the people of his Lord and Master without His presence. His language is, "O Lord, I am going forth to preach Thy gospel. Thou hast said in Thy Word, 'Lo, I am with you alway, even to the end of the world.' Lord, be with me. Lord, be with me. Make my heart to indite a good matter, and my tongue the pen of a ready writer. Enlarge my heart, give a door of utterance, clothe Thy word with power, that it may reach the hearts and consciences of Thy people, and that sinners may be converted unto Thee."

The Lord, thus working with them, confirms His word by the signs that follow. Paul was very sensible of the inability of the means of grace without the Lord's presence. Paul may plant, and Apollos may water in vain, unless God give the increase. In vain is Paul, or Apollos, or Cephas, or anything that man can do. It is by the Lord, and the Lord alone, working with His ministers in the preaching of the blessed gospel that sinners are converted and saints comforted. It is not by the minister's might and power, but by the might and power of the Lord. The Lord works with them. They have this treasure in their earthen vessels, that the excellence of the power may be of God, and not of them.

The Lord works by the ministry of the word, in enabling the man to preach the truth, and so to divide the word that each has his portion in due season. A portion is given to seven and also to eight. The lambs of the household, as well as the sheep, in the church of God, are edified, comforted, and built up. The minister not only wants to have it in his own knowledge and experience, but, when preaching, that the life and power may be felt in the souls of the people. Then, as Paul said to the Thessalonians, and which my soul longs to see and feel more of, "Our gospel came not unto you in word only, but in power." We ministers preach the gospel in *word only* when we are dry, shut up, and straitened. Then, there is no going forth; all seems dry and barren. What is this for? To teach us our own insufficiency. We cry to the Lord for His power, His blessed influence, to work by and with us, that some good may be done. We want the power. "Our gospel came not unto you in word only, but also in power, and in the Holy Ghost, and in much assurance."

IV. *"Confirming* the word with *signs following."* That is the confirmation of the word in the souls of them that hear it. How is it confirmed? One portion of the Word says, "To the law and to the testimony; if they speak not according to this word, it is because there is no light in them." What is this law? The Word of God, the blessed Bible. "The law of the LORD is perfect, converting the soul; the testimony of the LORD is sure, making wise the simple." If any man stands up to speak contrary to this, there is no light in him. "If any man speak, let him speak as the oracles of God. If any man minister, let him do it as of the ability which God giveth, that God in all things may be glorified through Jesus Christ." He is to minister as of the ability that God gives, not as man gives.

Take examples from the good ministers in the days of old, who proved all they said from the Word of God. The Bereans of old "were more noble than those in Thessalonica, in that they received the word with all readiness of mind, and searched the scriptures daily, whether these things were so;" whether they were in accordance with the Word of God. When this is done, the Lord is working by them; what they do is according to the law and the testimony. God's ministers have their sermons from the Word of God.

We sometimes sing hymns composed by Mr. Medley. We had in our church 40 years ago, a dear saint of the most high God, who heard Samuel Medley, who mentioned the following anecdote. A number of ministers were assembled for instruction, and Medley was present. An old minister who sat opposite to him in the room kept his eyes fixed upon him. At last, walking towards him, he took hold of his button, and said,

"Samuel, I have heard that you have begun to preach." Medley replied he had stood up sometimes to give a word of exhortation. The minister, who had been a long time in the work, said he would give him a word of advice. Medley said he would be glad of any advice from him. "Then my advice is this. Let the Bible guide you. Never attempt to preach to the Bible. Never try to make the Word of God say as you say. Go to the Lord, to a throne of grace, and what God gives from His Word, His blessing and approbation will be sure to follow." Thus God works with His ministers, confirming the word with signs following. To the law and the testimony. This is sound speech that cannot be condemned.

"The Lord confirming the word, with signs following." How is this done? Thus. The minister of God, in preaching His word, shows the sins and transgressions of His people, comes to their real state and condition as law-breakers, and shows the awful consequences of sin. The Lord works by him. The various portions of the Word the man of God brings forward are sealed home by the Spirit as a nail in a sure place. He describes the state and condition of a sinner; his weak, helpless, undone, lost state; the many vows and resolutions he has made and broken; so that he is brought to feel that if his salvation depended on his goodness, alas he never could be saved. He tells him from the Word of God that it is not works of righteousness he has done that will save him. He knows that if it depended upon his being saved by the law of works, he is utterly undone. Thus the word is confirmed. His mouth is stopped. He is brought in guilty before the Lord.

The invitations are, "Come unto me, all ye that labour and are heavy laden, and I will give you rest." "Ho, every one that thirsteth, come ye to the waters." "Whosoever will, let him come." "All that the Father giveth me shall come to me; and him that cometh to me I will in no wise cast out." These blessed truths are sealed and brought home with power; and the sinner's heart is fixed and encouraged. Thus the Lord works with His ministers, confirming the word with signs following. This is the confirmation these *spiritually* heavy laden and thirsty souls want; this sealing testimony of the Holy Ghost.

What are the signs following? When the preacher declares we are altogether in ourselves unclean, our righteousnesses are as filthy rags, the child of God says, "I know that is true what the dear man of God preaches." He then goes on to show that Jesus Christ is made unto us wisdom and righteousness; that He has wrought out and brought in an everlasting righteousness that will justify the sinner; that Christ is the end of the law for righteousness to the believer; and that this righteousness that Jesus Christ wrought out, God the Father imputes to the sinner. He brings forth Scripture to confirm it; and the Holy Ghost seals it home that Christ has done this *for me,* a poor guilty sinner: "Who of God is made *unto us* wisdom, and righteousness, and sanctification, and redemption." Thus the Holy Spirit applies the word, the Lord works with them, His ministers confirming and sealing the word spoken by the man of God.

Christ is the only sacrifice. No blood would atone for sin but the blood of the dear Redeemer.

> Not all the blood of beasts,
> On Jewish altars slain,
> Could give the guilty conscience peace,
> Or wash away the stain.

His blood is of a nobler and richer name than that of bulls and goats.

Thus the minister preaches the precious blood of the incarnate God as the church's redemption; the church redeemed by the precious blood of Christ. The Holy Ghost seals it home to the poor guilty sinner. The words are: "Deliver him from going down to the pit; I have found a ransom." The atoning blood of the Lamb is the ransom: "By the blood of thy covenant I have sent forth thy prisoners out of the pit wherein is no water." These are God's prisoners. They are delivered by the application of the blood of Jesus. The words of the minister are confirmed and sealed home. The child of God rejoices. These are the signs following.

When the man of God speaks of the efficacy of the blood of Christ, that it was not only the redemption price, but also a fountain to cleanse, as it is written: "In that day there shall be a fountain opened to the house of David and to the inhabitants of Jerusalem for sin and for uncleanness," the guilty sinner feels the efficacy of the blood of the dear Redeemer, which, applied by the Spirit, purges his conscience, and sins of a scarlet and crimson-like dye become white as wool. The atonement is sealed home and confirmed; and Christ becomes exceeding precious to the child of God. Thus God confirms the word by signs following.

Where God's ministers speak, the Lord causes the arrow of conviction to pierce the heart and conscience. No sooner does the sinner really feel the wound than he falls down, like Saul of Tarsus, with the cry, "Lord, what wilt thou have me to do?" What were the signs that followed the preaching of the gospel on the day of Pentecost? The Lord working with them, thousands were converted to God. When they went down to Antioch, the hand of the Lord was with them, and signs followed. Sinners were effectually called by divine grace. The Lord opens the ear. He gives the hearing ear, the seeing eye, and the understanding heart, as He did Lydia, so that she attended to the things spoken by Paul. The signs that followed Paul's preaching were that sinners were converted to God and effectually called by grace out of darkness into God's marvellous light. The Lord makes bare His arm in the gates of Zion, so that inquiring, seeking souls, with their faces Zionward, are encouraged. They are effectually called by God's grace, and born again of the Spirit: "Born, not of blood, nor of the will of man, nor of the will of the flesh, but of God."

We have great reason to be thankful that Zion is favoured with the gospel preached by His poor unworthy servants. We want to see more crying mightily to God to arise and build up Zion, that He would appear in his beauty and glory, and that His gospel may have abundant success.

"The Lord working with them, confirming the word with signs following."

What are the signs? I trust I am speaking to some this evening who, like myself, have been long bending their steps Zionward, who are far advanced in years. Our stay here will not be long. Then may we shine as lights in the world, so live that God may be honoured and glorified by our walk and conversation, remembering that we are not our own, but bought with a price, and therefore we should glorify God in our bodies and spirits which are His. We should shine as lights in the world, as a city set on a hill, that cannot be hid. "Let your light so shine before men, that they, seeing your good works, may glorify your Father which is in heaven." Such are some of the signs that follow the preaching of those whom the Lord has called to the work of the ministry. Amen.

4

Born of God

PREACHED IN ROCHDALE ROAD CHAPEL, MANCHESTER,
ON LORD'S DAY MORNING, JUNE 29TH, 1862.

*"Which were born, not of blood, nor of the will of the
flesh, nor of the will of man, but of God." (John. 1. 13.)*

The immediate connection in which these words stand is as
follows: Our Lord Jesus Christ, the promised Messiah, "came
unto his own, and his own received him not." By "his own" we
are to understand the whole of the Jewish nation, which are
nationally His peculiar people; He came unto them, but they
received Him not, but conspired against Him, and said, "This is
the heir; come, let us kill him, and the inheritance shall be
ours." Peter charges the horrid deed upon them; they "killed
the Prince of life;" but "as many as received him, to them gave
he power to become the sons of God, even to them that
believed on his name." None ever did, can, or will receive
Christ, believe in His name, and enjoy their relationship to a
covenant God as His sons, but such as are "born, not of blood,
not of the will of the flesh, nor of the will of man, but of God."

Paul draws a line of distinction between natural and spiritual
Israel: "They are not all Israel which are of Israel, but in Isaac
shall thy seed be called;" a remnant according to the election of
grace. So that whether Jew or Gentile, Barbarian, Scythian,

bond, or free, if they be the sons of God, by eternal adoption, they must in God's time and way be born again, "not of blood, nor of the will of the flesh, but of God."

In endeavouring to make a few remarks from the words we have now read, to the Lord's honour and our spiritual comfort and consolation and establishment in the truth as it is in Christ Jesus, we would notice three things.

I. The *necessity of the new birth.* The necessity appears from the solemn, important, and interesting conversation which took place between Nicodemus, a ruler of the Jews, and our Lord Jesus Christ. Nicodemus comes and speaks of the great miracles that the Lord had wrought, which were evident displays of His eternal power and Godhead. Our Lord makes no reply to Nicodemus in reference to the miracles that had been wrought by Him, but directs his attention to a great work, in which there is a greater display of His almighty power than in these miracles to which Nicodemus refers; and at once insists upon the new birth: "Verily, verily, I say unto thee, Except a man be born of water and of the Spirit, he cannot enter into the kingdom of God." (John 3. 5.)

Here the Lord insists on the necessity of being born again, and follows it up: "Marvel not that I said unto thee, Ye must be born again." The kingdom of God is a kingdom prepared by our heavenly Father, in which all His saints shall be landed safe, and appear for ever in His presence. And this kingdom shall be given to none but to those for whom it is prepared; and while the kingdom is prepared for a people, the people that are to be put in possession of it are prepared for the enjoyment of it. Hence we read of "vessels of mercy which he had afore prepared unto glory."

This preparation for immortal glory, commences in regeneration, in being born again, "not of blood, nor of the will of the flesh, nor of the will of man, but of God." It is impossible in every sense of the word, for an unregenerate person to enter heaven; it would be no heaven to him. He sees no beauty, no glory in, no need of, a precious Christ. The spirits of just men made perfect would be no company for him; he could not enter into their joys; there would be no comfort, no happiness, no bliss, no blessedness, no joy in heaven for him. I can recollect the time when the company and conversation of God's people, when the assembling of His saints, and the preaching of His gospel, were a burden to me. When I was compelled to attend, and be confined in the chapel, it was a prison to me, and why? Because when we are in a natural state we have no spiritual feeling, no spiritual desire, and see no beauty, no glory, no comeliness in a precious Christ. And, had we died then we had indeed died in our sins, not prepared for heaven, but prepared by our transgressions for destruction.

So, it is those who are born again by the Spirit of God, made new creatures in Christ Jesus, led by the Holy Spirit to see and feel the need of Him, to believe in Him, to glory in His Person, triumph in His finished salvation. These are the people who are born again, who love each other as members of the household of faith, who unite under the means of grace, and have a hidden melody in the heart, and can sing, "Hallelujah to God and to the Lamb," and can also join in the chorus, "Unto him that loved us, and washed us from our sins in his own blood, and hath made us kings and priests unto God and his Father; to him be glory and dominion for ever and ever. Amen."

Before I dismiss this branch of the subject, beloved, a solemn thought presents itself. Death and eternity are before us. Some of us are advanced in years; there can at the most be but a short space between us and the grave for the body, and eternity for the soul. The question arises in much solemnity, Are we, or are we not, born again of God? Are we, or are we not, in a prepared state for death and the kingdom? How frequently, when musing on this important subject, do the following lines drop into my mind:

> Prepare me, gracious God,
> To stand before thy face;
> Thy Spirit must the work perform,
> For it is all of grace.

II. The *power by which the great change of being born again is effected.* The evangelist in our text speaks particularly of this power, and in order that the transaction may shine the brighter and appear the more distinct, he couples three negatives with the positive declaration. Let us first notice the negatives, and then proceed to the positive.

We shall say a little upon the *negatives.*

I. "Which were born, *not of blood."* God's grace does not run in the blood from father to son. The abominable and filthy thing, sin, that our God hates, is hereditary; it runs in the blood from father to son. Adam begat sons and daughters in his own

image, as a depraved creature. How explicitly David speaks of
it. He says, "Behold, I was shapen in iniquity, and in sin did my
mother conceive me." How frequently is it seen that gracious,
God-fearing parents, parents that are born of God, have
profligate sons and daughters. See it in Eli; behold it in David;
and in many among ourselves. On the other hand, there are the
most profligate parents, whose offspring, born in actual sin and
transgression, have been, by the grace of God, regenerate and
made new creatures in the Lord Jesus Christ. See Abijah in the
house of an adulterous king, even Jeroboam. So that the Lord
has mercy upon whom He will have mercy, and compassion
upon whom He will have compassion. Our religion is therefore
not of blood, but by the teaching of the Holy Spirit of our God.

2. *"Nor of the will of the flesh."* What are we to
understand by the will of the flesh, in this portion of God's
Word? Paul, speaking of this subject, says, "I have great
heaviness and continual sorrow in my heart; for I could wish
that myself were accursed from Christ for my brethren, my
kinsmen, according to the flesh." His desire was that they
might be saved. As a Christian and a man of God he had great
desires for the spiritual and eternal welfare of those who were
allied to him by nature. We see this desire shine very
prominently on a very memorable occasion. Behold him
declaring what God had done for his soul in the presence of
king Agrippa and a splendid earthly court, before which he had
to appear as a witness for the precious name of the Lord Jesus
Christ. He speaks of the miraculous manner in which he was
converted and called to his apostleship; of the revelation of
Christ to his soul; of the preciousness of Jesus; and how he was
commanded to proclaim the glorious glad tidings of salvation
to perishing sinners. He also reviews the birth, sufferings,
death, and resurrection of Christ, and His ascension to glory;
and he declares these things are the records of heaven, and puts
it all to King Agrippa, who believed the prophets, and knew
that these things "were not done in a corner." Paul's powerful
language has an effect upon the king's mind, so that he
exclaims, "Almost thou persuadest me to be a Christian." Now
mark the feeling of Paul's mind. And Paul said, "I would to
God that not only thou, but also all that hear me this day, were
both almost and altogether such as I am, except these bonds."
Now we see the fleshly feeling and desire of the apostle was
such that he would, had it been in his power, have regenerated

the king and all that were then with him; but he could not reach the case; it required a greater Power.

Let us bring this down to our own feelings. Where is the minister that stands up to preach, that is concerned for the salvation of his hearers, who would not, if he could, carry the Word with power to their souls and convert them to God? Where is the God-fearing man, who has a wife that knows not the Lord, but is concerned for her to know God as her God? And where is the wife that has an unbelieving husband, but is concerned for his salvation? Where are the God-fearing parents who are not concerned for the salvation and welfare of their children? This is commendable so far as we view it subservient to the goodwill of Him that dwelt in the bush. We can do nothing without the Lord; it must be the power of God alone.

I have known individuals who had godly parents; their parents had been concerned for the spiritual welfare of their children, and their prayers had been bottled in heaven. The parents have died, and in God's own time answers to those very prayers have descended upon the offspring. Some of those offsprings have come to me in tears, and said, "O that I had those dear parents now, to tell them what God has done for my soul!" Such cases as these are an encouragement to use the means, leaving the result in the hands of our heavenly Father.

3. *"Nor of the will of man."* A great deal is said of man and of his free-will, we unhesitatingly grant; but what is that will free to do, while in a state of unregeneracy? The will is one of the faculties of the mind, a depraved faculty; so that men willingly drink in sin, like thirsty oxen drinking in water; they lie down, as thousands do as some of us did, in the sink of sin, and wallow in it and delight in it like a sow wallowing in the mire. Man's free-will in a depraved sinner leads him from God in the broad and downward road; it leads him to eternal destruction, if not prevented by the free and sovereign grace of God.

"O," says one; "has not man a will to choose the good and refuse the bad; to turn to God, and repent, and believe, and be saved?" We answer the question in the Lord's own way, and propose this question as a reply: "Can the Ethiopian change his skin, or the leopard his spots?" No; it is impossible; for, if so, "then may ye also do good, that are accustomed to do evil," So then, "it is not of him that willeth, nor of him that runneth, but of God that showeth mercy." Our salvation, our regeneration, is not to be traced to the will of man, but to the sovereign will of God. Mark the notable passage: "Of his own will begat he us."

Now let us look at the *positive* declaration. *"But of God."* O that we could pronounce this short sentence with the gravity and solemnity that its nature demands. "But of God." All human power must sink and die, "as a dim candle dies at noon;" and the great and almighty power of Jehovah, the Creator of heaven and earth, be exalted; for he is King of kings, and Lord of lords, above all praise and power, and above every name that can be named; and at the name of Jesus every knee shall bow, and tongue confess, that He is Lord.

Whoever is born again of the Spirit of God is regenerate; and, mark it: "Therefore if any man be in Christ, he is a new creature." There is a creation, a new creation. We ask the Christian, who can create but God? Man can perform wonders if you put something into his hand to work upon; but if he has nothing whereon to display his wisdom and demonstrate his handiwork he can do nothing. I was forcibly struck with this while walking through the International Exhibition in London. I beheld many things in the rough state as they were found in or on the earth, and I saw the wisdom and handiwork of man in bringing them forth to perfection, in a way that fills the mind with admiration. But had these men had nothing put into their hands to work upon, they could have displayed no power. So, none can create but God; and the same God, the same power displayed in the creation of the heavens and earth, is displayed in producing this new creation of grace in the soul of a sinner.

Paul, in speaking of this, says, "according to the exceeding greatness of his power." O the exceeding greatness of His power in the works of creation, and in the works of providence! But there is a greater display of Jehovah's power in the regeneration of one soul than in all the works of creation and providence. When the Lord by His almighty power spake the world into existence, there was none to oppose; He spake, and the thing was done. But in the regeneration of a sinner, there is an allied power fighting against the power of God; there is Satan, the god of this world, in the sinner's heart; there are the allurements of the world, all uniting to prevent the Lord from accomplishing the good pleasure of His will. But when the appointed time comes, the stronger man armed enters the sinner's heart; makes him willing in the day of His power;

brings down his lofty looks; abases his proud and hard heart; lays him in the dust and upon the dunghill, at the feet of a dear Redeemer; and He exerts His power, not by creature might nor by creature power, but by the power of God.

A sinner is born again by the power of God Himself. Sinners in a state of nature cannot take to themselves this power; they must be born of God. Lazarus had no power in himself to rise from the dead; neither had his sisters or friends any power to raise him. And we may further say, but with all solemnity, there was no power in the sighs, and groans, and tears of Jesus, as a man, to move Lazarus into life. Where is the power then? In Christ's eternal power and Godhead. Then behold it; He speaks the word: "Lazarus, come forth!" and we see the dead come forth, bound hand and foot in the grave clothes. So, when sinners are converted to God, the word of the Lord regenerates the heart as on the day of Pentecost. If we are born again it must have been the power of God to begin the work; the power of God to maintain it; and the power of God to complete it. If we have not the power of God, the soul is dead, religion is dead, and all is dead.

III.   Now let us proceed, in the last place, to notice *the marks and evidences of a sinner's being born again.*

Is it not a subject of vast importance to know whether we are born again? We all know we must die and that after death is the judgment; and if we are not born again, eternal destruction will be our destination. Whatever we may know, whatever we may profess, if we are not changed by divine grace we shall never enter into heaven; for the word of the Lord is explicit here. We must keep to the metaphor. Some people will have it religion begins in joy, and love, and peace. I have not so learned Christ, neither did Paul, nor the thousands at the day of Pentecost, nor the Philippian jailor; but more of this as we enter into the evidences of being born again.

1.   Look at it in the familiar style in which it presents itself to us. We must borrow from nature. When a child is born alive, as a token of its birth and the life of the child, *it is heard to cry.* When its cry is heard there is a token, an undeniable evidence, of the birth. Just so in a spiritual point of view. Men, before they are born again, may say prayers, make long prayers like the pharisees, or like Saul of Tarsus; but Saul never did cry, he never did pray spiritually, till Jesus met him on the way

to Damascus; not with offers and overtures that if he would turn, and repent, and believe, and so on, He would save him. My soul abhors offers and overtures made in this way, because, in its very language it tends to the exaltation of the creature and to the abasing of the mighty power of God. Christ met Saul of Tarsus with new covenant blessings in his own heart; such as, "I will and they shall." "Saul, Saul, why persecutest thou me? And he said, Who art thou, Lord? And the Lord said, I am Jesus, whom thou persecutest." And the Lord reached his soul with power; His arrow was powerful; Saul was humbled, and lay down at Jesus' feet. Now here we see the power of God. The Lord directs Ananias to go and speak words of peace and comfort to him.

All you that are born of God are praying souls; the soul born of God cannot live without prayer. God's sword is two-edged, cuts both ways. O that it may be so this morning! Have I any this morning that are careless and graceless? Have I any that are content and satisfied with a form of prayer in words, that pray not in their hearts? If so, God is against you. But if you are born of God you are a praying soul; you have inward sighs and groans because of your sin and sinfulness; you have spiritual hungerings and thirstings after Christ, and you cannot live without pouring out your heart and soul unto God. The Holy Spirit pours down into your soul a spirit of supplication and you are enabled to spread your case before Him, and your prayer is the prayer of the publican; and it will be your cry on your dying bed: "God be merciful to me, a sinner!" "Lord, save, or I perish!"

2. Let me notice another of the evidences of being born again. The apostle Peter uses the figure of a new-born babe: "As new-born babes *desire the sincere milk of the word.*" The God of nature has implanted in the very constitution of a new-born babe a desire for the breast and milk of its mother. See her take the babe; and with a mother's heart she clasps it in her arms and blesses it. This is an emblem; for so in grace; as sure as a sinner is born again of the Spirit of God, in the very constitution of that regenerated soul there is a spiritual desire, an inward thirst for the sacred Scriptures, for the preaching of the Word of God, for the company and conversation of the saints of God. Hence "we know we have passed from death unto life, because we love the brethren."

A person may be a new-born babe in Christ and yet be eighty

years old. I have some knowledge of a circumstance relating to this fact. Two men requested a neighbour of theirs, a grey-haired old man, to go and hear their minister. He strongly objected, and said, "Nay, nay. I was christened at church, confirmed at church, married at church, and I will be buried at church, and that is enough for me." They said they did not want to meddle with his church; but merely as neighbours, who had done him many a good turn, wished him to go to their chapel. "Well," said he; "you have done me many a kindness, and as one good turn deserves another, I will go with you." The time came, and they went, praying that God would bless the means to the conversion of the old man. Well; the minister drew the bow at a venture; the Holy Ghost caused the arrow to fasten in the man's soul, as a nail is fastened in a sure place. He went home, sat down, said nothing, looked into the fire, but could not open his mouth. His old wife said, "What is to do with ye?" He said, "I cannot tell; but yon man has said words that dropped into my soul." "O," said she. "I thought how it would be; they will make you as bad as themselves; but we will not leave our church." Another Sabbath came, and he went a second time. The Lord worked more powerfully the second time. He comes home at length, holds up his head, and looks at his wife: "I say, find me the old Bible." Here is a new-born babe in Christ wanting the Word of God. She looks upon the shelf, gets the old Bible, and rubs the dust off it. He reads here and there, page after page; at length he cries, "I say, is this the reet down owd Bible we have always had?" "Yes," she said; "we have never had any other." "Well," said the old man, "if this is the *own* (old) Bible, I have got *new* een (eyes)." O, yes, new eyes and a new heart, and the Lord worked powerfully.

As sure as a poor soul is born again of God there will be a thirst for God; I speak it experimentally. When my father insisted upon my reading a chapter on a Sunday night, and insisted upon my going to the house of God, I say it to my shame, I felt as if I could have cursed him in my heart, and I said, "If ever I become twenty-one years of age I will have my own way." But, bless the Lord, He will not let us have our own way; no; He will bring us to His feet with weeping and supplications. When the Lord laid hold of me what a thirst I had for the Word of God, for a prayer-meeting, and for the conversation of the saints. When we have a new heart, new desires, and new affections, we must walk in new ways.

See these marks confirmed by the apostle's declaration: "Therefore if any man be in Christ he is a new creature; old things are passed away; behold, all things are become new." What are these old things that must pass away, and the new things to come? When a sinner is born again he becomes a new creature; he cannot keep company with old companions any longer; he cannot walk any longer in his own sinful ways. O no; the grace of God has taken possession of his heart, and it never did and never shall fail to produce the effect God says it shall produce; namely, "teaching us that, denying ungodliness, and worldly lusts, we should live soberly, righteously, and godly, in this present world." The Lord hunts His people out, and brings them, with a broken heart and guilty conscience, to weep at His feet, and His words sound in their heart like an alarm: "Wherefore come out from among them, and be ye separate."

What a remembrance I had of this very passage last night. After tea I took a walk on Kersal Moor [where the Manchester races then took place]; went round the church, and thought of former times when I tried to run away from God. I got up early in the morning and went to the races. I got on the race ground; but O the misery and wretchedness and great terror my soul felt! I could no more abide in the camp of the wicked than I could cease to exist; necessity was upon me, and I looked to find a field where I might be alone, and pour out my soul to God. Heaven-born souls cannot revel and delight in sin. Sin lives in them, but they hate it, and abhor it; for if any man be born again he is a new creature. They are not of the world; God has called them out of the world, and they shall by the grace of God, show forth the praises of Him that hath called them out of darkness into His marvellous light.

Men regenerate of the Spirit of God have new views of themselves, and new feelings and new desires after Christ and His salvation, as the people of God, as His elect. Before my new birth, the people of God appeared to me poor melancholy fools, men of no pleasure and no enjoyment; and their prayers and talk were a plague and torment to me. But after God had wrought this change in my soul, and I was made alive from the death of sin, and I saw my need of a Saviour, I cried, "I will go with you, for I have heard that God is with you." And O what delight I took in the conversation of these very people I had turned my back upon. Thus there are new connections, new feelings, and new desires; old things have passed away, and all things are become new.

After this change had taken place in my soul, I once heard my mother talking to some people about me. She said, "I don't know what has taken place with our John; not long since he would never go to chapel; but now he is always with religious people, always going to chapel; there is quite a change in him." O, my friends, the sentence dropped from my mother's lips and sank into my heart, and I believe it will always be there: "He is always most happy when he is going with the old man." O what reason I have to thank God for the desire to go with the people of God, praying to be numbered with them in life and death and to all eternity. I sometimes think when Sunday morning comes, if some power were to compel me back to my old ways, what a hell it would be to my soul.

3. Now we have another evidence, which will lead us into the marrow of the gospel. The regenerate soul has *a spiritual appetite.* We have each a body, and a soul inhabiting that body. Now our bodies are earthly bodies, sensual bodies, for we were originally created out of the dust of the earth. Hence it is that the food the earth produces nourishes and strengthens our earthly bodies. The labouring man following the plough, or whatever labour it may be, perceives his strength fail, and he wants dinner time to come, that he may sit down at the table, and be refreshed in his body. The food he takes strengthens and refreshes him, and he is again able to follow his employment.

Look at one circumstance in the Bible. The prophet Elijah is fleeing from Jezebel; he comes to the wilderness, and sits down under a juniper tree, hungry and faint for want of food, and requested for himself that he might die; but the Lord sent His angel to him, with meat; and the angel said, "Arise and eat, because the journey is too great for thee. And he arose, and did eat and drink, and went in the strength of that meat for forty days and forty nights, unto Horeb, the mount of God" (1 Kings 19. 7, 8).

A man that is born again of the Spirit of God; can his soul feed and be satisfied with the luxuries the world produces? O no; let him have ever so splendid a table, and ever so much wealth, and heap upon him all the honours, titles, dignities, that a man on earth can bear, and in the heaven-born soul there is a vacuum, an aching void, that neither gold nor silver, nor wealth, nor dignities can fill. Do you want his song?

Were I possessor of the earth,
And called the stars my own,
Without thy graces and thyself,
I were a wretch undone!

What will satisfy a soul born again? We have a satisfaction, and that satisfaction is Christ. If we are born again of the Spirit of God, no provision will satisfy us but the Bread of eternal life, which comes down from heaven. Christ is the provision of the Father's house, and this provision alone will satisfy a heaven-born soul.

If you and I are born again of God we cannot be satisfied with the world and things of the world; and if you and I are born of God we are not, nor can be, satisfied in or of ourselves. I firmly believe from my own experience, that the longer a heaven-born child of God lives here, the more dissatisfied he will be with himself; the more he will sink in his own esteem; loathe and abhor himself, and repent, in his soul-feeling, in the dust before the Lord. On the other hand, if we are born again we shall feel a growing need of a precious Christ, of His glorious Person as the God-man and Mediator. We need Him as our covenant Head, and to feed upon Him as the mystery of godliness, God-man in the flesh, and we adore Him. We see Him fulfil the law of ten commands; we rejoice in His righteousness, and hunger and thirst after it. We also see Him in His blood-shedding; we see the work is finished, and our soul feeds upon a finished and complete salvation, all of grace, from first to last.

O, there is that in Christ that satiates the soul that is born of God. He is all and in all. It is of importance for you and me and every child of God to learn that He is our Saviour and Redeemer. We read in the prophecy by Ezekiel about a new-born babe being cast into the open field. O! How helpless it is! It can do nothing for itself; it must have all done for it. Now, if you are born again of God, you are yourself as helpless as regards saving yourself, and washing yourself from your sins, and clothing yourself in the robe of righteousness, and justifying yourself in a spiritual point of view, as that little child was. If we are born again we are like the babe cast out, helpless and crying, bewailing our condition, knowing that no man can help us. But when the Lord passes by, He spreads His skirt over us, and feeds and nourishes us with the Bread of heaven, and gives us all that we stand in need of. Heaven-born souls can do nothing for themselves. Christ and Christ alone is all and in all. Amen.

5

Believer's Baptism

PREACHED AT ZOAR CHAPEL, GREAT ALIE STREET, LONDON,
ON SUNDAY EVENING, MAY 22ND, 1853.

*"Can any man forbid water, that these should not be baptized,
which have received the Holy Ghost as well as we? And he
commanded them to be baptized in the name of the Lord."
(Acts 10. 47, 48.)*

Our text stands in inseparable connection with that
memorable event of the Gentiles being called by the grace of
God to a saving knowledge of the truth as it is in Christ Jesus.
The Holy Ghost had moved prophets to predict this hundreds of
years before the event took place; particularly the prophet
Isaiah, whose language we will read, as we shall see in the
connection of our text, its exact fulfilment. "Behold, I will do a
new thing; now it shall spring forth; shall ye not know it? I will
even make a way in the wilderness, and rivers in the desert."
(Is. 43. 19.) The wilderness here sets forth the Gentiles, and the
desert the heathen, in their fallen state. "The beast of the field
shall honour me, the dragons and the owls; because I give
waters in the wilderness, and rivers in the desert, to give drink
to my people, my chosen. This people have I formed for
myself; they shall show forth my praise." (Is. 43. 20, 21).
When the Lord's time came for the middle wall of partition
to be broken down between the Jew and the Gentile, He put His

fear into the heart of Cornelius, who was by nation and by
nature a Gentile. This man is particularly spoken of in
connection with our text. "There was a certain man in Caesarea
called Cornelius, a centurion of the band called the Italian
band, a devout man, and one that feared God with all his
house." The grace and the Spirit of God had evidently taken
possession of his heart and soul, and he "prayed to God alway,"
that he might be led and directed by Him. "He saw in a vision,
about the ninth hour of the day an angel of God coming in to
him, and saying unto him, Cornelius. And when he looked on
him he was afraid, and said, What is it, Lord? And he said unto
him, Thy prayers and thine alms are come up for a memorial
before God." (Acts 10. 1-4.)

Real heartfelt prayer never fails to be regarded by heaven.
"He will regard the prayer of the destitute." The Lord heard
the cry of Cornelius and answered his prayer and directed him
to send men to Joppa, and inquire at such a man's house for
Simon Peter, and to bring him into his house to blow the silver
trumpet of the everlasting gospel to Gentile sinners. The men
then set off and meanwhile God, who works "all things after
the counsel of his own will," was preparing Peter to receive
these messengers. He had been about his master's business; he
returned to his lodgings, and ascended to the top of the house,
where he often resorted for prayer and meditation. "And he
became very hungry, and would have eaten; but while they
made ready, he fell into a trance." Then he saw descending
from heaven a vessel "as it had been a great sheet knit at the
four corners," and in it were all manner of four-footed beasts
of the field, fowls of the air, and creeping things; and a voice
was heard saying, "Rise, Peter; kill, and eat." "Not so, Lord,
for I have never eaten any thing that is common or unclean."
"What God hath cleansed, that call not thou common." This
sheet was let down from heaven three times, and taken up
again.

What is to be understood by this? This sheet is a type of the
covenant of divine grace that is "ordered in all things and
sure." All the election of grace, Jew and Gentile, we have here
represented as being in the covenant safe and secure. Be it
observed, they all came down from heaven in the sheet; not a
single creature got out. O no! God's elect can never get out of
His heart; never get out of the finished salvation of Jesus
Christ; never perish. And there is another memorable thing,

and that is, that none were put in. Universal charity can never put a soul into the covenant of grace, can never bind up one in the bundle of life who has not been bound there by the threefold cord of a triune Jehovah.

I once made these very remarks in Halifax, about 20 years ago. There was a lady present, and she said, "I believed it to be true; but I thought I had no mark and no evidence of being one of these creatures in the covenant;" and she went home greatly bowed down in her soul. She then had three restless nights and days. Her husband wanted to know what was the matter, and she could not tell him. The servants also wondered what was the matter with their mistress, going about as she was with tears trickling down her cheeks, and sighing and groaning in her soul. She went to bed the third night with this important subject on her mind, and she said, "I reasoned in the following manner: 'What am I? A poor, sinful, guilty, vile creature? What have I done ever to merit God's mercy and favour? Nothing at all; and if He were to mark my iniquity, and send me to hell, He would be just right.' I then felt a breaking in my spirit, a humiliating feeling of my own unworthiness; tears trickled down my cheeks, and I cried, 'Dear Lord, I am the clay, and Thou art the potter; I deserve nothing but damnation; and if Thou shouldst save my soul, if I am in this sheet, it is all of Thy rich, sovereign grace.' " She afterwards sent for me, and said, "The love of God was shed abroad in my soul; I had the testimony from the Lord that I was indeed in this sheet, and I rejoiced and triumphed in the God of my salvation, till nature overcame me, and I fell asleep. When I awoke in the morning, it was with the consciousness that I was in the sheet, in the covenant." Glory was in her soul, and glory upon her countenance. Her husband and her family wondered at what had taken place, for she went about her family affairs singing the song of free, everlasting grace.

Now, while Peter was thinking of this vision, and wondering what it could mean, the Lord said, "Get thee down; there are certain persons waiting for thee at the door." He then went down, and inquired whence the persons came, and what was their errand. They rehearsed the circumstances to him, and he went with them, doubting not that God's hand was in it. When he arrived at the house, Cornelius came out, received him with a glad heart, and fell down, and would have adored him; but, says Peter, "No, no; I am a sinful man, having like passions with yourself; worship not me, but my Master." He then went into the house, and inquired wherefore he was sent.

There is one remark here that we may notice by the way. When he went into the house, the family and friends were all ready waiting to receive him and to hear what God would say to them. How well it looks on the Lord's Day morning to see people gathered together, like Cornelius and his household, to hear the word of the Lord. When Cornelius had stated all the circumstances of the case, Peter said, "I perceive that God is no respecter of persons, but in every nation, he that feareth him, and worketh righteousness, is accepted with him." Peter had up to this period believed that God respected the Jew in preference to the Gentile. Now he saw that this was done away with. He did not mean to say that fearing God and working righteousness were the grounds of our acceptance. O no! We are accepted in the beloved; our fearing God and working righteousness are fruits and effects of that enjoyed in the soul.

Peter now proceeds to blow the jubilee trumpet of a free-grace salvation among the Gentiles, preaches the glory of Christ, His solemn death for the sins of His people, and His resurrection from the dead. He exalts the sin-atoning Lamb; and the word that went forth from his lips was carried by the power of the Holy Ghost into the heart of Cornelius, and of his household, and his friends; the word had free course and was glorified. Peter and the brethren saw that the word was received with joy and gladness, probably from the tears that ran down their cheeks, and the glow of animation that was perceivable on their countenances. Peter saw that there was the dew of heaven, the savour of life, and the power of divine truth felt in the souls of the people; and seeing this he exclaims, "Can any man forbid water, that these should not be baptized, which have received the Holy Ghost as well as we? And he commanded them to be baptized in the name of the Lord."

These are the circumstances connected with the important words of our text. We have here two main things:

I.   *The characters who have a right to the ordinance of baptism.*

II.   *The command that is given.*

I.   *Who are they that have a right to the ordinance,* that are commanded to be baptized? If we refer to John's baptism, none were admitted to that ordinance (save the Lord of life and glory) but such as were *penitent.* When the seed of Abraham came and desired to be baptized by John, and gave no evidence of repentance, he said, "O generation of vipers, who hath warned you to flee from the wrath to come? Bring forth fruits meet for repentance." None have a right to the ordinance of baptism but those who know what it is to have a godly sorrow for sin. These Gentile sinners had repentance granted unto them, for it is said concerning them that the apostles "Glorfied God, saying, Then hath God also to the Gentiles granted repentance unto life." Are we penitent, friends? Do we know what godly sorrow for sin is? that repentance that needs not to be repented of? If we do, the grace of God is in our heart; the privileges of God's house are our own. But if we are strangers to this, the command of God does not come upon us.

With regard to those who have a right to the ordinance of baptism, look at the commission given by our Lord to His disciples, before His ascension to glory, and we shall there find who they are to whom the Lord directed His disciples to administer baptism. The evangelist Matthew renders the commission as follows: "And Jesus came and spake unto them, saying, All power is given unto me in heaven and in earth." This is a solemn and great truth. O what a help have I found this truth to be to my soul, that my Lord and Master has all power in heaven and in earth! "Go ye, therefore, and teach all nations, baptizing them in the name of the Father, and of the Son, and of the Holy Ghost; teaching them to observe all things whatsoever I have commanded you; and lo, I am with you alway, even unto the end of the world." So then, they that have a right to the ordinance of baptism, and are commanded to be baptized, are such as are *taught of God.* God's ministers are appointed to teach sinners as God guides and directs; and as the Lord honours their teaching, and makes them wise unto salvation by faith in the Redeemer, they are to be baptized in the name of the Saviour. Advocates for infant sprinkling reverse the Master's order; they say, "Baptize them in their infancy, and teach them afterwards." This is not the true state of the case. None have a scriptural right to the ordinance but such as are taught of God. "It is written in the prophets, And they shall be all taught of God. Every man, therefore, that hath heard and hath learned of the Father, cometh unto me." It is the soul that has fled for refuge to the Redeemer, that has been cleansed by the blood that flowed from Emmanuel's wounded side, that has the privileges of the ordinances of God's house.

The evangelist Mark renders the commission in the following memorable language: "And he said unto them, Go ye into all the world, and preach the gospel to every creature." Why is the gospel to be preached in all the world and to every creature? Because God's elect are scattered abroad amongst the various nations of the earth; and the Lord has ordained the ingathering of His elect by the ministration of His word. Paul preached to Jews and Gentiles, "and as many as were ordained to eternal life believed"; for "faith cometh by hearing, and hearing by the word of God." He that believeth and is baptized shall be saved, but he that believeth not shall be damned." No unbeliever has a right to the ordinance; the command does not go to them; it commands them that believe to be baptized, and to show their love and attachment to Christ by bowing to His sceptre.

The apostles of Christ thoroughly understood their Master's commission, and acted upon it. Thus on the day of Pentecost, when Peter stood up and preached to the people, the word dropped from Peter's mouth, and was carried by the Holy Ghost into the heart and conscience of guilty sinners. Hence it is said that they were pricked to the heart; conviction was wrought by the Spirit of God, and they cried out, "Men and brethren, what shall we do?" Peter says, "Repent, and be baptized every one of you in the name of Jesus Christ for the remission of sins." As Peter preached, in that memorable sermon, Jesus Christ and Him crucified and the resurrection from the dead, the power of God attended the word not only to convince, but to conquer and to edify; for it is said, they that gladly received His word were baptized." Mark it; they received the word of free, finished salvation with joy and gladness. Christ was present to their souls; the love of Christ was shed abroad in their hearts, and they were baptized, and the same day were added to the church. We see then who are commanded to be baptized.

Philip preached the gospel to the Samaritans: "And when they believed Philip preaching the things concerning the kingdom of God, and the name of Jesus Christ, they were baptized, both men and women." We read of the Ethiopian eunuch; "What doth hinder me to be baptized?" "If thou believest," says Peter, "with all thine heart, thou mayest." And the eunuch said, 'I do believe.' I believe in the name of Jesus

Christ; I feel that I love him, and I like to honour Him and show forth His praise, See, here is water; what doth hinder me to be baptized?' On a confession of His faith He was baptized in the name of the Lord. It is a great mercy to come under that character!

We read that there were households baptized; and of the gaoler it is said, "He believed in God with all his house;" but there is no account of there being infants in any of the households that were baptized in the apostolic age. Our friends, however, who vindicate infant sprinkling, say they suppose there were infants in those households. I never had yet, and I hope I never shall have an article in my creed, a doctrine in my theory, that is based on supposition. We must have a "Thus saith the Lord" for our faith, and the example of Christ and His apostles for our practice, or our faith is not sound, and our practice is not according to godliness.

Two men were disputing on the ordinance of baptism; one of them contended that the children of believing parents had a right to the ordinance in preference to others, and the other contended that all children should be baptized alike. A third person who listened attentively to the arguments on both sides, said at length, "It appears to me that you miss one very important principle in the debate." "What is that?" they said. "Why, the sign of the cross upon the forehead," alluding to the practice of the Church of England. Both disputants said, and with some warmth, "Where do you find the sign of the cross mentioned in Scripture?" "Well," said he, "You show me the chapter and verse where you find infant sprinkling, and in the very next to that you will find the sign of the cross." The two men looked at one another with surprise, for they could find neither chapter nor verse for sprinkling infants, and the man came off victorious. "To the law and to the testimony; and if they speak not according to this, it is because there is no light in them. " It may be said, "Have there not been good and gracious men advocates for infant baptism?" I believe there have and there are some to this day. But we are to follow great and good men only so far as they follow Christ and His apostles. When we see a great man, be he churchman or dissenter, going contrary to the Scriptures, let us never follow him a yard; let us follow the Master, and act according to His practice and the practice of primitive Christians. "Can any man

forbid water, that these should not be baptized, who have
received the Holy Ghost as well as we?"

Again, None have a right to the ordinance of baptism unless
they are *made partakers of the Holy Ghost.* Every elect vessel
of mercy in regeneration is made a partaker of the Holy Ghost:
"Know ye not that your body is the temple of the Holy Ghost,
which is in you?" What are the marks and evidences of those
that have the Holy Ghost? If we have the Holy Ghost dwelling
and working in us, and teaching us, we see and feel our lost,
ruined, helpless state and condition. Now as this is an evidence,
my conscience bears me witness that I have this evidence of
being a partaker of the Holy Ghost, and have had it for the last
forty years. Have you got this evidence? There is another
evidence. If we are saved, it must be owing to the covenant
engagements of Christ, through the incarnation of Christ who
came into the world to save the chief of sinners, through the
justifying righteousness of Christ, through the atoning sacrifice
of Christ, through the resurrection of Christ who was
"delivered for our offences, and raised again for our
justification," through the ascension of Christ, and by virtue of
our union to Christ, pleading our cause above. Now, we bring
one portion of God's word to crown these remarks: "Jesus is
able to save to the uttermost." Do you believe it? Is it precious
to your souls? "Able to save to the very uttermost all that come
unto God by him." Lost, to be saved; naked, to be clothed;
filthy, to be washed in His blood; weak, to be strengthened;
ignorant, to be instructed; — "able to save to the very
uttermost all that come unto God by him, seeing that he ever
liveth to make intercession for them." Now every man (I do
not care to what sect, or party, or denomination he belongs)
who is a partaker of the Holy Ghost, is made to cleave to the
Person of Christ, and to the efficacy of His blood and
righteousness, with a full purpose of heart, with Paul's
determination to know nothing but "Christ, and him
crucified." Where these feelings are, the Holy Ghost has
produced them. "Can any man forbid water, that these should
not be baptized, which have received the Holy Ghost as well
as we?"

Some years ago our church was in a great difficulty about
receiving a young girl sixteen years of age, who had been
brought up amongst us. Her father was a member, and she had
been in a Sunday school. She intimated to her friends what was

on her mind; but the visitors who waited upon her did not give her any encouragement, knowing the slippery path of youth, especially in some of the northern districts, where some who had come into church from the Sunday school brought disgrace and reproach upon the cause of religion. We tried to put her off and asked her to wait a year or two and see how things went on. She told us what she felt of her own sinfulness and wickedness and of her need of Jesus Christ. When I talked to her about being put off, she said, "Well, parson," (for that is what they generally call me,) "if you think I have not received the Holy Ghost, to make me acquainted with my sin and my need of Jesus Christ, you may put me back; but if you think I have been made a partaker of the Holy Ghost, and am taught by Him, as I trust I am, then does it not say, 'Can any man forbid water, that these should not be baptized, which have received the Holy Ghost as well as we?'" The church was completely locked fast; the father wept; and we all said, with one voice, "Jane must be baptized." Ah! where the Holy Ghost dwells in the heart, who can forbid water, that they should not be baptized?

II. Now, let me say a word as to the *command itself:* "And he commanded that they should be baptized in the name of the Lord." The command was given by Peter; but it is the command of the Master; Peter and his brethren received it from Christ Jesus, the great Head of the church, the King of kings and the Lord of lords. So the Lord speaks from the pulpit tonight by His ministering servant, commanding every soul who has received the Holy Ghost, to come forward, if he has not already done so, and be baptized in the name of the Lord. O that the Lord would carry the command home into some of your hearts! There are some individuals among you who, I believe, love the Lord Jesus Christ, and see and feel your need of him and His salvation. Have all my friends who love my Lord and Master obeyed his command? Have you all obeyed it? It is just the same at home. Last September I baptized an old friend of mine whom I had known forty years, in his seventy first year; and the dear man of God was under the necessity of coming forward because he could stay no longer. O that the Lord would lay this with a solemn weight upon the consciences of such as love Him! The Saviour says to them, "If ye love me, keep my commandments; thus shall all men know that ye are my disciples, if ye do whatsoever I command you." "If I am

your Lord and Master, where is your fear, and reverence, and
honor of me, if you live in disobedience to my command?" O
Lord, may Thy Spirit come with power into the minds of these
Thy children, and may they be led to put on Christ by an open
profession of His name by baptism!

What is meant by being baptized? "And he commanded
them to be baptized in the name of the Lord." Baptism, when
applied to Christ, the great Head of the church, means His
solemn and awful sufferings in the garden of Gethsemane, and
on Calvary's cross. Hear His language: "I have a baptism to be
baptized with; and how am I straitened till it be
accomplished!" He alludes to His overwhelming sufferings in
the garden of Gethsemane, and on the cross of Calvary, when
His garment, or vesture, was dipped in His own blood. Dr.
Watts sings,

> Thy body slain, sweet Jesus, thine,
> And bathed in its own blood,
> While all exposed to wrath divine,
> The glorious Sufferer stood.

And shall we be ashamed to be baptized in water, when we take
a view of our Master being baptized for our sins in His own
blood?

Again, baptism, in reference to Christ, sets forth His death
and burial. We are said to be buried with Christ by baptism,
and to be baptized into His death. When Jesus had died for our
sins, His body was taken down from the cross, and laid in the
sepulchre; and the angel said, "Come, see the place where the
Lord lay," pointing to the grave and the tomb. Now I can say
to this congregation typically, "Come, see the place where the
Lord lay," (pointing to the baptistry.) The burial of Christ,
then, is set forth by this ordinance, and also the resurrection of
Christ from the dead: "If ye, then, be risen with Christ;" "Now
is Christ risen from the dead, and become the first-fruits of
them that slept."

The ordinance of baptism, in reference to the church of
God, sets forth something of an experimental character very
strikingly. In the first place, as baptism is a burial, it is not
according to things to bury anyone until he is dead. No living
person is put into the grave and buried. In like manner, no
sinner has a right to the ordinance of baptism until he is dead. I
speak not of the death of the body. Of what death, then, do I

speak? That death of which the apostle speaks: "I was alive without the law once; but when the commandment came, sin revived, and I died." It is the soul that is dead to the law, dead to all hope of salvation and justification by works of righteousness. Are you dead, my friends? If you are not dead in this sense, you have no right to the ordinances of God's house; the command does not belong to you.

About eighteen years ago, when I was labouring amongst you here. I met an aged pilgrim in a narrow passage, quite unexpectedly; and having shaken hands with me, he said, "I hear you are going to baptize before you leave the town." "Yes," said I, "I am; on Thursday night." Then, in a rather sharp and hurried manner, he said, "Well, Sir, are you going to baptize the dead or the living?" The question came to me in a rather novel form, and I was for the moment at a loss for an answer. After a short pause, however, I saw the old man's design; and I said, "I hope I am going to baptize both the living and the dead. They are dead to all hope of saving themselves by works of righteousness; they are alive to God by faith in the Lord Jesus Christ." "Go on, Kershaw," said the old man, "baptize dead and living, and God will bless you."

If we are dead *and* living in this sense, the ordinances of baptism and all the privileges of God's house belong to us. In the believer being baptized, he shows to the world and the church that he is dead to the world's follies and vanities, dead to all hope of saving himself; that his spiritual life is hid with Christ in God; and that he wishes to live the rest of his days to the honour of the great Jehovah, and to follow the Lamb whithersoever the Lamb goes. Christ, we read, went into the river Jordan, and was there baptized of John; and the believing soul wants to follow Him there; he wants to take up his cross, and follow the dear Redeemer through good report and through evil report.

> Dare to defend his noble cause,
> And yield obedience to his laws.

I was brought up an infant sprinkler, and I was very much prejudiced in favour of my own principles. I well remember the first time I saw the ordinance of baptism administered according to the word of God. The sermon had no effect upon my mind. I quibbled at all the man said; but when I saw him come out of the vestry, the persons to be baptized following him, and heard him speak a few words to them, and then saw him baptize them, the impression was made upon my mind, "This is the baptism of the Bible;" and I have thought so from that very moment up to this day. It is the way of the Master; it is the way of the apostles; it is the way of the church of God that walks in the ordinances of the Lord's house as they have been delivered by our Lord and Master and by His servants.

Now, it may be that there is some living soul here who says, "I believe the ordinance is right, and that what the Scriptures say, and what you have been saying about it, is all right." Then I say, if you have not been baptized, why do you not come forward and bow to the sceptre of King Jesus? You say, perhaps, "I have my reasons." Well, what are they? "In the first place, I have seen and heard of several who have come forward and been baptized, and they have not worn well; they have fallen into sin, have disgraced their profession, and been a trouble to the church of God." Now do not be offended at me for using Scripture language, and saying, "What is that to thee? follow thou me." "Well," you say, "I should not like to bring reproach upon the cause of God." So far as there is a tender principle in your breast for God's honour and glory, and for the purity of the doctrines and practices of God's church and people, I revere it; but then, in the midst of your scruples there is another principle that we cannot for a moment countenance, — a distrust in the power and ability of the Lord to keep you. Venture into His hands, weak and helpless; rely on His promise that He will "keep the feet of his saints;" call upon His name, "Lord, help me to stand my ground, to persevere and endure unto the end." "Yea," He says; "I will; I will uphold thee with the right hand of my righteousness." Venture into the Lord's hands; give yourselves up in the first place to Jesus, and to the church of God in Jesus' name. For Paul said, in reference to the church at Corinth, "They first gave their own selves to the Lord, and unto us by the will of God." This being done, my friends, let the believer bow to the Master's sceptre by being baptized in His name, and thus obey the great command. Amen.

6

Finishing Our Course With Joy

PREACHED AT HOPE CHAPEL, ROCHDALE, MARCH 3RD, 1867, ON COMPLETING
THE FIFTIETH YEAR AS THE PASTOR OF THE CHURCH.

My dear and esteemed Friends, — You are aware that it is now fifty years since I became the pastor of the Church of Jesus Christ worshipping within these walls. Though so long ago, I have a lively remembrance of all the circumstances of importance connected with that memorable day. The text the Lord laid upon my mind to preach from on that occasion was a prayer of David's and it was also my earnest, fervent desire, as recorded in Ps. 118. 25: "O LORD, I beseech thee, send now prosperity." When I look back at the past, I have abundant reason, with David, to say, "I love the LORD, because he hath heard my voice and my supplications. Because he hath inclined his ear unto me, therefore will I call upon him as long as I live." Bless the Lord, peace and prosperity have attended us, both temporally and spiritually, of which I hope to speak more particularly on another occasion.

On the present opportunity I feel it my privilege to call your attention to a portion of the word of God which has long been on my mind to speak from at this time.

"But none of these things move me, neither count I my life dear unto myself, so that I might finish my course with joy, and the ministry, which I have received of the Lord Jesus, to testify the gospel of the grace of God." (Acts 20.24)

The middle clause of the verse more especially is what has been most upon my mind: *"So that I might finish my course with joy."* The whole verse contains great and precious truth, both in doctrine, experience, and practice, sufficient for many sermons. By way of introduction, with the help of the Lord, we will briefly notice the preceding part of the verse: "But none of these things move me, neither count I my life dear unto myself." Kept by the power and grace of God, none of the severe persecutions and afflictions Paul had been called to endure for conscience or for his Master's sake moved him from the truth as it had been made manifest in his soul by the power of the Holy Ghost. Through grace, he rejoiced that he was counted worthy to suffer shame for the sake of Him "who endured such contradiction of sinners against himself," that dear Lord whom he so furiously persecuted in the persons of His saints; He who had stopped him in his mad career when he was running headlong to everlasting misery and destruction. When some concerning whom he had hoped well, and who for a time did run well, turned aside to error and others into open sin, he was sorely grieved, and wept for the reproach they brought upon themselves and the cause of God and truth, as was the case with some at Philippi. (See. Phil. 3. 17-19.) But none of these painful things moved him from his attachment to his Lord and Master and His people, but made him the more earnestly pray that they might "press toward the mark for the prize of the high calling of God in Christ Jesus" and have their "conversation in heaven, from whence also we look for the Saviour, the Lord Jesus Christ."

My dear brethren, like Paul and many others of the Lord's ministers, I have had my sorrows on account of some who have caused me and the church under my care much trouble. But instead of being moved from my steadfastness, I saw the necessity of being able to stand more firmly in the evil day, and having done all to stand. I have seen the beauty, propriety, and seasonableness of the exhortation given by the apostle to the Corinthians: "Therefore, my beloved brethren, be ye steadfast, unmoveable, always abounding in the work of the Lord; forasmuch as ye know that your labour is not in vain in the Lord." (1 Cor. 15. 58.) The cry of my soul has long been, "Dear Lord, give thy poor unworthy servant grace to obey this exhortation."

The apostle adds, in the next clause of our text: "Neither

count I my life dear unto myself." We are not to conclude from these words that the apostle did not set a proper value upon his life as being the gift of God, and that he was careless and indifferent about it. His desire was that he might not live to himself in the enjoyment of worldly ease and earthly honour, but with Moses choosing rather to suffer affliction with the people of God than to enjoy the pleasures of sin for a season. He lived in the blessed persuasion of what he wrote to the church at Rome: "For whether we live, we live unto the Lord; and whether we die, we die unto the Lord: whether we live, therefore, or die, we are the Lord's." (14. 8.) He knew that he was not his own, but was bought with the price of the precious blood of Christ, and his desire was to live so as to glorify God in his body and spirit, which are his; and, from the love he felt to his Lord and Master, he was willing to lay down his life for His sake. This is evident from his own words, as in Acts 21. 11. When the prophet Agabus took Paul's girdle and bound his hands and feet, and said, "Thus saith the Holy Ghost, So shall the Jews of Jerusalem bind the man that owneth this girdle, and shall deliver him into the hands of the Gentiles." The brethren hearing this begged and entreated the apostle, with many endearing arguments and tears of affection, lest they should be deprived of his valuable life and labours, not to go up to Jerusalem. But mark well the apostle's answer, which demonstrates that his Lord and Master's honour was dearer to him than his life: "What mean ye to weep and to break mine heart? for I am ready not to be bound only, but also to die at Jerusalem for the name of the Lord Jesus." And when he would not be persuaded, they ceased, saying, "The will of the Lord be done."

We now come to the apostle's earnest and fervent desire to finish his course with joy. And what a union do I feel with Paul! Truly we are brethren. It has long been my desire that God would give me grace, as he did his servant Paul, that I may fight a good fight and keep the faith till my Lord shall call me home to dwell with Him in glory.

    I.   We will first make a few remarks upon the *course*.

    II.   The desirableness of *finishing our course with joy*.

    I.   Fallen man, dead in trespasses and sins, is walking according to the course of this world, according to the prince of the power of the air, the spirit that now worketh in the children of disobedience. In the first three verses of Ephesians 2 I see my own state and condition accurately described, the course I was pursuing in the broad and downward road which would have led me to destruction had it not been for the grace of God putting a stop to my sinful course.

> O to grace how great a debtor,
> Daily I'm constrain'd to be.

I apprehended that Paul had in view his course, both as a Christian and a minister of the gospel. He looked back to the day of his effectual call by grace, when he had to leave his former friends and pursuits, and was made willing to serve Him he had hated and despised; when he was enabled in the Lord's time to put on Christ by faith, and then made an open profession of the same by being baptized in the name of the Holy Trinity. He remembered his entrance on the work of the ministry, the many trials and sorrows that had beset his path, and the supports and consolations that he had received of the Lord to enable him to hold on and preach Christ as the new and living way that leads to eternal life. His desire was to hold on to the end and finish his course with joy, as is evident from the language of our text: "That I may finish my course with joy, and the ministry which I have received of the Lord Jesus, to testify the gospel of the grace of God." He had the answer of a good conscience that he had served the Lord with all humility of mind, and with many tears and temptations which befell him by the lying in wait of the Jews, and how he had kept back nothing that was profitable. (See verses 19, 20.) The apostle could appeal to the elders at Ephesus that he had not shunned to declare unto them the whole counsel of God; for wherever he went he was enabled faithfully to preach repentance towards God and faith in our Lord Jesus Christ as inseparably connected with the enjoyment of salvation. He was also concerned to maintain a conscience void of offence, both towards God and man. He was ever desirous to cut off all occasion of the adversaries speaking reproachfully of God and truth, and to be an example to the believer in every good word and work, giving full proof that he was not coveting the fleece, but seeking to feed the flock of God which He hath purchased with his own blood, coveting no man's silver, or gold, or apparel, but working with his own hands that he might minister to his own necessities and to those of them who were with him.

My dear friends, pray that the Lord may make His ministers like Paul, with an eye single to His honour and glory, with a deep concern for the peace and prosperity of Zion, the furtherance of the gospel, and the gathering together of the children of God that are scattered abroad.

Paul's course had been a painful one to flesh and blood (see 2. Cor. 11. 23-28); yet he was not weary of his Master's service. He pressed forward, looking unto Jesus, the Author and Finisher of his faith, believing he should be more than a conqueror through Christ that loved him.

II.   We now come to the second part; the desirableness of *finishing our course with joy*. The Lord, before whom I now stand in this large and attentive congregation, is witness that I have many times upon my knees, in the course of my ministry, read the chapter from whence my text is taken, especially from verse 17 to the end, begging and beseeching the Lord that I might follow the example of Paul and all the apostles, so far as they followed Him, who has given us an example that we should follow His steps. My desire has long been that I might not only preach the gospel, but live as it becometh the gospel, crying daily to the Lord, "Hold thou me up, and I shall be safe;" "Keep thou me by thy power, and I shall be kept." The prayer of David in Ps. 17. 5 has often been pleaded by me before the Lord: "Hold up my goings in thy paths, that my footsteps slip not." Also the last clause of the prayer of Jabez: "And keep me from evil, that it may not grieve me," wound the minds of the brethren, and open the mouths of the enemies of God and truth, causing them to blaspheme. The Lord knows that I have many times told Him that I would rather die than bring a reproach upon His cause. The late William Tiptaft used to say, "It is a good thing to be well laid in the grave;" which is a sentence full of meaning and importance. He always used to pray that we might not sin cheaply.

When I am led to look back and call to remembrance the way the Lord has led me in the wilderness, not only forty years, but sixty years, — for it is now that time since He put His fear into my heart, — the expression of my soul is, "Having, therefore, obtained help of God, I continue to this day." The language of John Newton is often on my mind:

Many days have passed since then,
Many changes I have seen,
Yet have been upheld till now;
Who could hold me up but thou?

How seasonable is the exhortation: "Let him that thinketh he
standeth take heed lest he fall." The advice given in 1 Kings 20.
11 is good: "Let not him that girdeth on his harness boast
himself as he that putteth it off."

I am now in my seventy-fifth year, and in the fifty-fourth of
my ministry, and by the grace of God which has been given me
have stood upon the walls of Zion with an unblemished
reputation, often calling to mind the exhortation: "Be ye clean
that bear the vessels of the Lord." (Isa. 52. 11.) I know that the
Lord has given me favour in the eyes and hearts of many who
love the doctrines of sovereign, discriminating grace which I
have long preached, and which many say lead to sin; but, bless
the Lord, they have thus far led me *from* sin and to desire
holiness. But I would rejoice with trembling, knowing that, if
left to myself, through the evils of my heart, the allurements of
the world, and the temptations of Satan, I might in an
unguarded hour do that which would be as the dead fly in the
apothecary's ointment, — cause my name to stink, instead of
being, as the wise man said, "better than precious ointment." I
would be daily looking to the Lord for the fulfilment of that
precious promise that I am often pleading before Him: "He
will keep the feet of his saints." The words of Paul to Timothy:
"And the Lord shall deliver me from every evil work, and will
preserve me unto his heavenly kingdom, to whom be glory for
ever and ever, Amen," have been a great comfort to me of late.
(2 Tim. 4. 18.)

In my younger days I did not think so much of the prayer of
David in Ps. 71. 9 as I do now: "Cast me not off in the time of
old age; forsake me not when my strength faileth;" so that, as
the outward man perisheth, I may be renewed by the grace of
God in the inner man day by day, bring forth the fruits of
righteousness, that my last days may be my best days, and that,
like Paul, I may finish my course with joy, and hear the Lord
say, "Well done, good and faithful servant. . . . enter thou into
the joy of thy Lord." (Matt. 25. 21.) That Paul finished his
course with the felt joy of God's salvation in his soul is evident
from his own words to Timothy: "For I am now ready to be
offered, and the time of my departure is at hand. I have fought

a good fight, I have finished my course, I have kept the faith; Henceforth there is laid up for me a crown of righteousness, which the Lord, the righteous judge, shall give unto me at that day: and not to me only, but unto all them also that love his appearing." (2 Tim. 4. 6-8.) The blessed anticipation of these things made him ready and willing to lay down his life for the sake of Him who loved him and had done such great things for him, to show forth His honour and glory and His faithfulness and ability to succour and support in the time of trial for the comfort of others who might live after him, and the confounding of the enemies of God and truth. He believed that Jesus Christ, who had loved him and given Himself for him, would grant him grace to enable him to endure to the end, and that when absent from the body he would be present with the Lord.

Whatever joy a sinner may have in the prospect of death and eternity, if it does not arise from a view by faith which is the gift of God, of his interest in the Person, work, and finished salvation of our Lord Jesus Christ, it will be like the hope of the hypocrite spoken of in the book of Job. It will perish at the giving up of the ghost. Beloved, how needful it is to examine ourselves as to the ground and foundation of our joy and rejoicing. Is Christ our "All and in all," in His glorious Person, as the God-man Mediator in the perfection of His obedience, as our law-fulfilling righteousness, in His great atoning sacrifice for our sins upon the cross, by which the curse of the law is for ever removed? Our blessed Jesus, having abolished death, and brought life and immortality to light by the gospel, swallowed up death in victory; which caused the apostle triumphantly to say, "O death, where is thy sting? O grave, where is thy victory? The sting of death is sin; and the strength of sin is the law. But thanks be unto God which giveth us the victory through our Lord Jesus Christ."

The desire of my soul is to die rejoicing that God's just and holy law, broken by me in thought, word, and deed, has been fulfilled for me by my Lord and Saviour Jesus Christ. The language of Paul on this subject has long been sweet and precious to my soul. Writing to the Corinthians, he says, "But of him are ye in Christ Jesus, who of God is made unto us wisdom, and righteousness, and sanctification, and redemption, that. . . . he that glorieth let him glory in the Lord." It also rejoices my heart to feel and see that all my sins were removed by Christ our spiritual scapegoat; so that when they are sought for they can never be found.

How desirable in the prospect of death to have the testimony of the Holy Spirit in our soul that we are delivered from the curse and condemnation of the law. I hope never to forget the time of my deliverance out of bondage, and being brought into the liberty wherewith Christ has made me free, the following portion of God's word being blessedly applied: "There is therefore now no condemnation to them which are in Christ Jesus, who walk not after the flesh, but after the Spirit. For the law of the Spirit of life in Christ Jesus hath made me free from the law of sin and death." I could then rejoice that my name was written in heaven in the Lamb's book of life, and say with Job, "My record is on high" and "I know that my Redeemer liveth." It was Paul's joy that he knew in whom he had believed; and he had the happy persuasion that Jesus, in whom he believed to the saving of his soul, was able to keep that which he had committed into his hand against that day. I have often said amongst you that this blessed portion of the word of God enters into the vitality of true religion in the soul of a sinner. All my hope and trust are in the Lord, into whose hands, by the grace of God, I have committed my cause. I cannot find language to describe the comfort and support I have enjoyed from these words:

> If I am found in Jesus hands,
> My soul can ne'er be lost.

I know that I lay dead in trespasses and sins, and that the Lord quickened my soul, which is an evidence of eternal life. He has solemnly declared that none to whom He gives eternal life shall ever perish, neither shall they be plucked from His hands. Paul not only rejoiced in the ability of Christ to save to the uttermost all that come to God by Him, but in His ever living to make intercession for them. Is it not our joy that we sinners have an Advocate with the Father, Jesus Christ the righteous? The following lines have often dropped into my soul with great power and sweetness:

> He lives! he lives! and sits above,
>   For ever interceding there;
> Who shall divide us from his love,
>   Or what shall tempt us to despair?

It is for our comfort the Lord has said, "Because I live, ye shall live also." It is a great blessing to know we are "dead to the law," and that our spiritual "life is hid with Christ in God."

Whilst in this time state we look, by faith, in the glass of God's word, and see our Lord Jesus Christ enthroned in glory, with all power both in heaven and earth in His hands, as Head over all things to His body the church. His ministers, whose feet are "beautiful upon the mountains" of His precious truth, are to say unto Zion, "Thy God reigneth," and that He will see that all things shall work together for His honour and the good of all who love Him and are the called according to His purpose. These lines are the joy and comfort of my soul:

> Jesus, the King of glory, reigns
> On Zion's heavenly hill;
> Looks like a lamb that has been slain,
> And wears his priesthood still.
>
> He ever lives to intercede
> Before his Father's face.
> Give him, my soul, thy cause to plead,
> Nor doubt the Father's grace.

How many of you, my hearers, feel a response in your souls to the last two lines just cited? Had I as many souls to be saved as there are stars in the firmament, I would commit them all into my Redeemer's hands, who has engaged to present me faultless before the presence of His glory, with exceeding joy. I would not cast away the confidence I have in Him for a thousand worlds. In Him I have everlasting consolation and good hope through grace, which is as the anchor of my soul, sure and steadfast, which enters within the veil, where Christ the Forerunner is for us entered. Having, like Paul, committed the cause of my soul's salvation into Jesus's hands, I earnestly desire to finish my course with honour to His name, and that an abundant entrance may be ministered unto me into His everlasting kingdom.

My dear hearers, are you satisfied with the form of religion, a regular attendance upon the means of grace, a knowledge of the truth in the theory, without feeling any influence on your souls? I am greatly concerned about many of you who have been brought up amongst us, and are traditionally attached to me as a minister and the people that meet to worship the Lord in this place. My soul longs to see the word preached confirmed in your hearts by the power of the Holy Ghost, with signs following, such as a heartfelt, godly sorrow for sin, and a spiritual hungering and thirsting after Christ and His righteousness. Where there is no spiritual mourning over sin and longing for Christ and His salvation, there is no spiritual life in the soul.

The grace of God planted in the heart is a well of living water, springing up into everlasting life. Bless the Lord, I have long felt the springing up of this living water within me, and well know it is His gift, as He said to the woman at Jacob's well (Jn. 4. 14). I long to see it in others, and the love of Christ constraining them to say with David, "Come and hear, all ye that fear God, and I will declare what he hath done for my soul."

I have reason to be thankful that the Lord has in some measure honoured His own truth spoken by me to the conversion of sinners to Himself, turning them from darkness to light, and from the power of Satan unto God, as many of you can testify who are now present, and who, by the grace of God, have given yourselves to us as a church in the fear of the Lord. We have experienced many refreshing times at our church meetings, in hearing sinners give a reason of the hope within them, with meekness and fear; and seeing, as Barnabas did, "the grace of God in them" (Acts 11. 23); and, like him, we have been glad. My soul has often been encouraged when portions of the word of God have been spoken of that I have preached from, which have been honoured of God, in convincing of sin, stripping and humbling the sinner, in comforting and encouraging the fearing, timid, doubting soul, the delivering of them out of bondage into the liberty of the gospel by an application of the precious blood of Christ by the power of the Spirit, and in establishing them in the truth as it is in Jesus.

We can also call to remembrance the many blessed refreshing seasons we have enjoyed while attending to the ordinances of the Lord's house, — baptism and the supper of the Lord, when we have sung with melody in our hearts:

> With pleasure we behold
> Immanuel's offspring come;
> As sheep are gather'd to the fold,
> And left no more to roam.

and while sitting around the table of the Lord in commemoration of the solemn sufferings and awful death of our Lord Jesus Christ, in whom our hope for heaven rests. Many times have we been greatly blessed while singing the hymn after supper:

How sweet and awful is the place,
With Christ within the doors

especially verses 3, 4 and 5:

While all our hearts and all our songs
Join to admire the feast,
Each of us cry, with thankful tongues,
Lord, why was I a guest?

'Why was I made to hear thy voice,
And enter while there's room,
When thousands make a wretched choice,
And rather starve than come?'

While singing these lines, my soul has often said with great humility and thankfulness, "Ah, Lord, if it had not been for thy almighty, efficacious, all-conquering, discriminating grace, I should rather have starved than come." With great joy, therefore, have I joined in singing the next verse:

Twas the same love that spread the feast,
That sweetly forced us in;
Else we had still refused to taste,
And perished in our sin.

While I am speaking to you of these seasons, I think of many that have joined with us on these occasions who have been removed by death, who were very near and dear to us in the bonds of the gospel. They have finished their course with joy, and are now uniting with the spirits of just men made perfect in singing the everlasting song: "Salvation to God and the Lamb." My soul is ready to say,

When shall the day, dear Lord, appear,
When I shall mount to dwell above,
And stand and bow amongst them there,
And view thy face, and sing, and love?

We have been spared many years together, and the Lord has done great things for us, whereof we are glad. According to the course of nature, my stay amongst you below cannot be very long; but my prayer is often to the Lord that you may be preserved faithful to the truth and the ordinances as they have been delivered unto us, and that when I have finished my course as a minister and under-shepherd amongst you, the great Head of the church will raise up one to go in and out amongst you of His own fitting and qualifying, of good report, and able to trace out the footsteps of the flock, setting before you the things that he himself has seen, and looked upon, and handled of the word of life.

May the Lord bless what has been delivered to our soul's comfort, for His name's sake. Amen.

7

Seeing Jesus

PREACHED AT ZOAR CHAPEL, GREAT ALIE STREET, LONDON
ON THURSDAY EVENING, APRIL 28, 1848.

"But we see Jesus." — (Heb. 2. 9.)

I would call your attention to three things arising from these words.

First, let us endeavour to describe the *characters* who see Jesus. *Secondly let us take notice of the person seen — Jesus.* And *Thirdly* I shall make a few remarks upon *the place* where He is to be seen. "But we see Jesus."

I. — In the *first* place, we have to take notice of *the characters who see Jesus spiritually.* Observe the term used, "We see Jesus." He is to be seen only by the eye of living faith. No man can see Jesus spiritually without he is made a partaker of the Spirit and grace of God. "The natural man receiveth not the things of the Spirit of God; for they are foolishness unto him; neither can he know them, because they are spiritually discerned." (1 Cor. 2. 14.) But Jesus and the things of Jesus, are spiritually seen and discerned by God's spiritual people. Man in a state of nature without the quickening influence of divine grace in his soul, may see Jesus speculatively and nominally; he may see Him with a theoretical knowledge as He is set forth in the Bible as Saviour and Redeemer; but he cannot see Him spiritually without living faith. Balaam saw Him in a natural sense, and spake glorious things concerning Him; but Balaam did not see Him with the spiritual eye of faith as connected with the salvation of his soul. He had a consciousness of this; hence he says, "I shall see him, but not now. I shall behold him, but not nigh." His conscience told him that he should see Jesus as an angry judge, which made him tremble and desire that he might die the death of the righteous, and that his last end might be like theirs. But his heart bore testimony against him that he did not want to live the life of the righteous, nor have the grace of God in his heart as they do. He never saw by faith the Lord Jesus Christ as his Saviour and Friend, nor as the Redeemer of his soul.

No man ever did, ever will, nor ever can see Jesus really and truly as He is, and enjoy His preciousness, but those who are brought to see and feel their need of Him. Sinners, naturally dead in sin, must be made spiritually alive before they can see Jesus. A sinner in a state of nature is in a state of darkness. Darkness covers the great deep of his heart; and gross darkness the minds of the people. "Once ye were darkness," says the Apostle, "but now are ye light in the Lord." While a man or woman remains dead in sin, in a state of darkness and alienation from God, though he or she may be a vessel of mercy, and may have a personal interest in the salvation of Jesus, yet they never can see the Person of Christ nor the glory of Christ till divine life and light is communicated. The Lord Jesus Christ is to them while in this state, as the Prophet Isaiah describes a root out of a dry ground: without form or comeliness; and when He is seen, there is no beauty in Him that He should be desired. (Is. 53. 2)

Here I remember my own case, and how it was with me in my own heart. I look back at the place where I was when God first arrested my conscience—the state I have been attempting to describe was my condition before the Lord. I was in a state of death, darkness, blindness, ignorance, carelessness, and indifference; seeing neither suitableness, beauty, nor glory in the Lord Jesus Christ why I should be concerned about Him.

"But we see Jesus." When the Holy Spirit takes possession of a sinner's conscience; gives him to see his sin, guilt, blindness, ignorance, and darkness, and causes him to feel what a rebellious, lost, ruined, and undone sinner he is; what a transgressor and law-breaker he is before the Lord; all hope and expectation of saving himself is at once cut off by God's holy law. Yet the poor soul, all the time he remains under these spiritual convictions, does not see Jesus as His Saviour and Redeemer; he is as Paul writes to the Galatians, "shut up unto the faith which shall afterwards be revealed." He now sees only his sin, guilt, and misery; he discovers only an angry God in a broken law: he knows himself only as a vile transgressor, an enemy, and a rebel. He feels that he has sinned against heaven, and in the sight of the Lord, and that he is not worthy of the least of God's mercies; and what to do, or where to go, he cannot tell. His soul is all but sinking into despair; so that at times he wishes that he had never been born, or that he was not possessed of a never-dying soul. Darkness is on his mind in reference to how God can be just, and yet the justifier of such a sinner as he sees and feels himself to be. But the Holy Spirit gives this soul a glimpse of Jesus; this inspires hope, and a ray of encouragement is communicated to his waiting heart.

The Holy Ghost never did, nor will He show such a sinner an end of perfection in himself and bring him into needy circumstances in his feelings before the Lord, and then leave him there. O no; that soul shall have an earnest and fervent cry put into his heart for help and salvation. The Holy Spirit will lead him to wrestle and plead with the Lord at the footstool of mercy for a discovery of Jesus to his conscience. When the Lord speaks by His Spirit in His word to this poor soul, He says, "Look unto me, and be ye saved, all the ends of the earth; for I am God, and there is none else". "A just God and a Saviour; there is none beside me." The man may have been trying to save himself, but he could not: all he could do was to sink deeper into despondency and misery; so that at length he becomes afraid lest the pit should open its mouth on him, and swallow him up. Many in this state of mind have been so deeply exercised with these feelings that they have been afraid to close their eyes in sleep lest when they awake they should open them in the pit of perdition.

When the Holy Spirit leads the soul to see how the Lord Jesus Christ has espoused his cause in covenant and counsel, in the ancient purposes of His love; when He works faith in his heart to receive this glorious truth, and applies it with divine power to his soul, then he feels a happy liberty. Faith comes by hearing, and hearing by the word of God; and now the soul finds the truth of this blessed declaration, that "This is a

faithful saying, and worthy of all acceptation, that Christ Jesus
came into the world to save sinners." These are sinners who are
sick of sin, who are sorrowing on account of it, whose hearts
are full of despondency and disquietude, and who want the
manifestation and revelation of the blood of Jesus to be applied
to their wounded consciences. When the Holy Ghost enables
the soul to look by faith to the ability, the willingness, and the
all-sufficiency of Jesus to save to the uttermost all that come
unto God by Him — what a blessed sight it is to him! what a
heart-cheering, soul-ravishing, Christ-exalting view it is to his
soul! Then he sees that the Lord Jesus Christ is the highway of
holiness; that He is a glorious way; a way whereby God can be
just, and yet the justifier of all those who believe in Jesus; a way
in which sin is taken away with all its damning consequences,
the law with its curse removed, justice satisfied, and hell and
destruction everlastingly defeated. When the believer is led to
see and feel these things, how he delights in Jesus! Jesus
becomes precious and "altogether lovely" to his never-dying
soul. This is seeing Jesus my friends. "But we see Jesus."

II. — We come to the *second* branch of the subject: *the
person seen* — Jesus. "We see Jesus." The very name of Jesus
to the eye and ear of faith has a blessedness and preciousness in
it. It is the most sweet and blessed name given under heaven.

> How sweet the name of Jesus sounds,
> To a believer's ear!
> It soothes his sorrows, heals his wounds,
> And drives away his fears.

> (J. Newton)

The Person seen by the eye of faith is Jesus. When the angel
announced to Mary that she should conceive and bring forth a
son, it was told her that his name should be called Jesus. He is
the promised Messiah — the Ancient of Days — the Bright and
Morning Star — the Branch which should come out of Jesse's
rod — the Sun of Righteousness that should arise with healing
in his wings — the Seed of the Woman who should bruise the
serpent's head — the Immortal Word that was made flesh, and
dwelt amongst us — the Child born, the Son given, whose name
is Wonderful, Counsellor, the mighty God, the Everlasting
Father, the Prince of Peace, and upon whose shoulders the
government of all things in heaven and earth is placed — the

King of kings, and Lord of lords! This is He, at whom devils fear and tremble. O, this is the glorious Person seen — the Lord Jesus Christ, in whom all fulness dwells, and who is head over all things to His body the church. Adored be His name, He is "over all, God blessed for evermore."

Why shall His name be called "Jesus"? There is a blessed and powerful reason why this name should be given to Him, and that is, "because he shall save his people from their sins." Not make them an offer and proffer of salvation, if they will accept His mercy and His grace. O no, the Lord Jesus Christ went to the end of the law for righteousness for every one of His people. The Lord's testimony by the mouth of the angel was, that He should "save his people from their sins." The Father gave Him to the church in covenant counsel for this very purpose before the world began; hence He says, "All mine are thine, and thine are mine, and I am glorified in them."

We see Jesus our Redeemer, then, as Saviour from sin; and a blessed sight it is to the household of faith to see Him in this glorious character. He is the Saviour of poor, lost, ruined, and undone sinners. There is nowhere else the sinner can look to for rest, peace, joy, or comfort to his soul, but to the Lamb of God which taketh away the sin of an elect world. The Holy Ghost leads every one of the chosen vessels of mercy to know something of what I am talking about.

Peter felt this in his heart and soul. There were many who followed Jesus only for the loaves and fishes; but He said to those characters, "No man can come to me, except the Father which hath sent me draw him:" and again, "Except ye eat the flesh of the Son of man, and drink his blood, ye have no life in you." But these mere letter professors of religion did not much like this doctrine of election and predestination; and therefore we read, "From that time many of his disciples went back, and walked no more with him. Then said Jesus unto the twelve, Will ye also go away? Then Simon Peter answered him, Lord, to whom shall we go? thou hast the words of eternal life." As though Peter should have said, 'There is no other Saviour but Thee, Lord; there is not another name given under heaven whereby we can be saved but Thine. We have tried other refuges, O Lord, but they have all failed; and we have now followed Thee as a matter of necessity. We are deeply dyed and stained with sin, and we cannot save our own souls; but we look to Thy precious blood to wash our sins away. We have no worth or worthiness of our own to plead, but we look to Thy righteousness alone for justification. Such being our state and case, O Lord, to whom can we go? to whom can we look but unto Thee? for Thou alone hast the words of eternal life: Thou, and Thou alone, art exalted as a Prince and a Saviour to give repentance unto Israel and remission of sins.'

Now this is seeing Jesus. Have you seen Him? If so, you have had a glimpse of His beauty: you have felt the need of His great salvation, and seen His suitability and preciousness to your case and circumstances: you have had pantings and longings for faith's view of His glorious Person. This is seeing Jesus: and such knowledge of Him is eternal life. These feelings are not wrought by nature, but they are all the effect of the grace of God in the heart. "But we see Jesus."

This Person is not only called Jesus; but the Holy Ghost calls Him also in the scriptures, "Jesus Christ," or "Christ Jesus our Lord." Whoever sees Jesus high and exalted, sees Christ. In the constitution of His Person as God and man in union, He is Immanuel, the anointed of the Father; the Son of man whom He has made strong for Himself; mighty to help, save, and deliver guilty sinners who cry to God for salvation. When the soul feels himself so sinking and helpless, and so low that he cannot help or raise up himself or his brother, how sweet it is to have faith's view of this blessed and mighty Person. He knows that God's ministers cannot help or raise him up, only as God works by them. He rejoices that his help comes from a more blessed source; from the Lord of hosts, the great Creator of heaven and earth. This is the Christ of God, the Lord's anointed. That precious text, "I have laid help upon one that is mighty," has done my soul good many times, when I have felt myself so weak and helpless; to know that I have such a mighty Saviour, Helper, and Deliverer. This glorious Person is Jesus, the Christ of God, the anointed of the Father, the Redeemer of the church, who is strong and mighty to save.

The believer not only sees Him by faith, but he feels Him precious too. It is useless to see Him merely in the judgment, and never feel the life and power of His salvation in the soul. But whenever a believer enjoys the blessed influences of the Spirit in his heart, he more than sees Jesus; the sight lifts him out of his sin and wretchedness, raises him from his legal workings and gloomy fears, and gives him blessed evidence in his own soul that this person is Jesus, the Christ of God, by the might of God's grace, and the glory of His power.

"We see Jesus" when we see Him as Lord of all. "Ye call me Master and Lord; and ye say well; for so I am." He is the Lord God omnipotent, who lives and reigns in the high court of heaven; whom angels worship and adore, and whom they delight to honour and obey. Jesus Christ, our Lord and Master, is worshipped and adored by ransomed spirits before the throne, who cast their blood-bought crowns at His precious feet, and crown Him Lord of all. He is worshipped and adored by holy and elect angels, who never left their first estate. His glorious Person is seen in that world of bliss and blessedness in all His beauty and immortal grandeur. Our Lord and Master is "King of kings, and Lord of lords." He is the blessed and only Potentate, by whom kings reign and princes decree justice. He has this blessed and noble appellation given to him, "Prince of the kings of the earth." (Rev. 1. 5.) The Father says of Him, "Yet have I set my king upon my holy hill of Zion." He reigns also in the hearts of His children; grace reigns in them through righteousness unto eternal life. Wherever grace reigns in the heart, it will reverence and obey the Lord's precepts and commands. If He is your Lord and Master, you will delight to fear, reverence, and obey Him in all His appointed institutions.

Our blessed Jesus is seen and felt to be Lord of all by the children of God. He is Lord of all their afflictions and trials; He reigns over men and devils; and He has declared that nothing shall hurt or harm them; and that "No weapon that is formed against thee shall prosper; and every tongue that shall rise up against thee in judgment thou shalt condemn." When He sends forth His ambassadors to publish good tidings of peace upon the mountains of Zion, they are to say to His church and people, 'Fear not: thy God, thy Saviour, thy Redeemer lives and reigns.' Yes; bless His precious name, He not only reigns over all in heaven, but He reigns over all in earth, and over all the affairs of His church. This oftentimes enables us to praise Him with our heart and soul, that whatever events may transpire will serve to shew forth His glory in the salvation and spiritual welfare of His church and people, which made the Apostle to say, "All things work together for good to them that love God, to them who are the called according to his purpose."

This is Jesus, the Christ of God, our Lord and Master, whom

we worship and adore. Have you seen Him, my friends? 'Ah,' says one, 'I hope and trust I have seen a little of Him; but it is only a little.' Why, those who have seen the most of Him have had but a little sight of His majesty and glory; they have seen Him only through a glass darkly; but the time will come when they shall see Him in open vision without a veil between. Some one may say, 'I hope and trust I have seen a little of the beauty of Christ; I see my own need and destitution; I feel my lost, ruined, and undone condition. But I want to see more of the Lord, and to enjoy more of Him in my soul. I want to get nearer to His heart; and to love, honour, and glorify Him more.' Such a soul as this is made honest by the grace of God. He has seen Jesus to be his Lord and Master; he is drawn and attracted to Him as steel is to the loadstone, the Holy Spirit working in him to will and to do of His good pleasure. "But we see Jesus."

III. — In the *third* place, let us *notice the place where Jesus is to be seen.* "But we see Jesus." Though we may have spiritual eyes given us to see the Lord Jesus Christ, and be blessed with a very strong sight to see an amazing long way backwards and an amazing long way forwards; yet, if I may use a metaphor for illustration's sake, we cannot behold Jesus without a telescope is given us to see with. That telescope I hold in my hand — the word of the Lord! Jesus is seen by the eye of faith as He is set forth in the word of God's grace.

We observe in reference to the place where Jesus is seen — that He is seen with the spiritual eye of faith in the secret counsels of eternity, in the vast covenant settlements of the eternal Jehovah. David saw Him in the everlasting covenant on his dying bed; and the sight of Jesus as his covenant Head cheered and refreshed his soul in the prospect of dissolution. He says, "Although my house be not so with God, yet hath he made with me an everlasting covenant ordered in all things and sure." Jesus is seen as the covenant Head of His church. The Father chose and ordained the church to life and salvation in Christ before the foundation of the world. The blood of Jesus is seen to the eye of faith to be the blood of the covenant; and His righteousness is the righteousness of the covenant.

Faith sees the Lord Jesus Christ as espousing the cause of His church and people by assuming their nature, in being made of a woman and made under the law, that He might deliver them from all their miseries and woes, and all the awful consequences connected with their fallen state. Faith beholds Jesus taking their sin and guilt into His own hands, and putting it away for ever. It assured them of their everlasting interest in Him, and that He will raise them up from the depths of sin and hell to the highest bliss in glory. Thus the believer sees how Jesus has espoused His cause in the counsels of eternity. It is a soul-ravishing sight, and it has done my soul good many a time, when by faith I have been enabled to see how Christ has united Himself to my person in the everlasting covenant ordered in all things and sure; how He has taken my cause into His hands, and how He has established it on better promises than the old covenant. He will never fail. If He make a promise, He will be sure to fulfil that promise in the experience of His people. I seldom stand up to preach but what this comes to my mind: God says, "He shall not fail nor be discouraged, till he have set judgment in the earth." (Isa. 42. 4.) He shall not fail in accomplishing the salvation of His people; He will finish the work which the Father gave Him to do.

"But we see Jesus." We see Him in the types and shadows, and in all the promises and prophecies made concerning His coming in the flesh. He is seen in His incarnation. Time would fail us in tracing the holy life and history of our Lord Jesus Christ. Let us therefore call your attention to some of the most important places where Jesus is seen by the household of faith.

He is seen spiritually by a living faith. When a sinner is convinced of sin by the work of God's law on his conscience, he will generally be going about to establish a righteousness of his own. But when the Spirit of God brings him into bankruptcy, gives him to see his guilt, and causes him to feel its workings in his heart, then he wants to see Jesus who has redeemed him from it, and gone to the end of the law for righteousness to every one that believeth. Faith traces Jesus in His pure and perfect life from the manger to the cross; but beholds nothing but fire and destruction in God's holy and righteous law. Heaven is well-pleased for His righteousness' sake; He has magnified the law, and made it honourable. The soul sees in the Lord Jesus Christ a justifying righteousness. This righteousness is imputed by God the Father to him; and the soul receives it by precious faith, and glorifies in the perfect obedience of the Lord Jesus Christ. The believer is complete and accepted in Jesus; and he stands before the eyes of infinite Purity in Jesus all fair, without spot, blemish, or any such thing;

and though in himself he is as black as the tents of Kedar, yet in the Lord Jesus Christ he is all comely and all fair. He sees that in Jesus he has a law-fulfilling righteousness; and as he beholds it, he sees such a glory in it, that he bursts out with the church of old, "Surely shall one say, in the LORD have I righteousness and strength." Or again, "My soul shall be joyful in the LORD; I will glory in the God of my salvation." It is here that you see Jesus is made your law-fulfilling righteousness.

Do you desire to see Jesus by precious living faith? Do you hunger and thirst after Him? Do you earnestly pray to be found complete and accepted in Him? If so, you have seen Jesus: and the sight of Him has done your soul good. When we see Jesus made sin for His church and people, we see Him in very solemn and awful circumstances. When by faith we view Jesus in His agonies and sufferings, we are able to enter into that prophecy, "They shall look upon me whom they have pierced." The Lord is determined that His people shall see Him in the garden of Gethsemane as a suffering Saviour, oppressed and labouring under the weight of their sin, and enduring the contradiction of sinners against Himself; resisting unto blood, striving against sin. Jesus must be seen nailed to the accursed tree, expiring as a spectacle to angels, men, and devils.

"As Moses lifted up the serpent in the wilderness, even so must the Son of man be lifted up, that whosoever believeth in him should not perish but have everlasting life." Jesus must be seen lifted up and exalted on the cross. Look at the type. The Israelites were suffering under a dreadful malady in the wilderness, and were in dying circumstances. Moses is directed to make a serpent of brass, to erect it on a pole, and make this proclamation throughout the camp, that whosoever shall look to the brazen serpent shall be healed of his malady. The antitype says, "So must the Son of man be lifted up," that whosoever looks to Him by faith shall be saved from the malady of sin. Some may ask, "Why is the type used a serpent? It is contrary to the nature of the meek, lowly, and immaculate Jesus to be typified by a serpent. There was no guile found in His mouth, wherefore then should the antitype be prefigured by a serpent?' It is to set forth the evil and malignity of sin, and to show that it has its origin from the old serpent, the devil. It is a truth big with comfort to the household of faith, that when Jesus hung upon the cross He was a pure, holy, innocent lamb in Himself; but as He was suspended there, with the guilt and sin of His church and people imputed to Him, enduring the curse of the divine law, bearing their sins and transgressions away, and delivering them from Satan the old serpent, He was made a curse for them. Though Jesus was perfect innocence itself, yet sin and iniquity being imputed to Him upon the cross, He bore the tremendous curse due to sin, and atoned for it on the accursed tree.

As Jesus is seen by faith in His blood-shedding and sacrifice, in His solemn and awful death, enduring the curse of the law and bearing away the multiplied transgressions of His people; as He is seen exalted on the cross, making an end of sin and bringing in everlasting righteousness; while the soul is looking to Jesus by faith, and gazing on Him in His awful and solemn sufferings, he loses the burden of sin from his conscience; he loses his doubts and fears; he sees Jesus made sin for him, removing the curse of the law. While a sinner looks to Jesus thus by precious faith the devil flees away. The Devil cannot stand his ground when the soul is gazing by faith on Immanuel on the cross; he loses his chains and his fetters, and is brought into sweet and blessed liberty. He sees that He who was rich, for his sake became poor, that he through His poverty might be made rich; that He died the just for the unjust, to bring sinners to God; that He died for their offences, and was raised again for their justification. This is a most solemn sight, a most humbling sight; yet at the same time a most soul-comforting, heart-cheering, God-honouring, and Christ-exalting sight. Everyone who has seen Jesus thus by faith is sure of immortal glory.

O that we may see more and more by faith our Jesus suffering and dying on the cross for our sins, and rising again for our justification! O that we may have more fellowship with Him in His sufferings! O that we may look more and more unto Him; and in looking feel our burdens fall off, and enjoy sweet peace, pardon, and liberty in our conscience! Before we are enabled to look to Jesus, all is darkness and misery; but in proportion as we are looking to Him, we shall be delivered from our darkness and gloominess. The more Jesus is seen by faith, and revealed to the heart, the more will His beauty and preciousness be seen, and the more will the soul delight in Him as the altogether lovely, and the chiefest among ten thousand.

"We see Jesus." He is seen in the tomb. When Jesus entered the grave, all the sins and iniquities of His church and people were buried in the tomb with Him to rise no more. Jesus was laid in the grave in death's cold embrace, the same as His people: but with this difference; we sleep to rise no more till the resurrection morn; but our victorious and conquering Head burst the barriers of the tomb on the third morning. He put away our sin, endured the curse, satisfied law and justice, vanquished death and hell, brought life and immortality to light, and rose triumphant over death, hell, and the grave. Our Jesus is seen in His immortal triumphs as conquering all our foes. He is the spiritual Samson, who has overcome all the enemies of His church and people. It is a blessed sight to see our risen and exalted Lord! He became the first-fruits of them that slept. As sure as Christ our covenant head arose from the dead in victory over all His enemies: so sure shall every elect vessel of mercy not only be raised from a death of sin and iniquity to live a life of faith upon the Lord; but when He comes the second time in His triumphant glory, all the members of His mystical body shall rise up fashioned like unto His glorious body, and live and reign with Him in blessedness for evermore. The resurrection of Christ is not only a "lively hope" to our souls; but it is "a good hope through grace," which we would not give up for a thousand worlds. Sometimes I see and feel such a beauty in it that I would not give it up for a million worlds. If we were to give that up, we should have no anchor for our vessel in the storm and the tempest. We can never give up our hope; it is an anchor to the soul, both sure and steadfast, and it enters into that within the veil whither the Forerunner is for us entered. That hope lays hold of a precious Christ. We are saved by hope. We follow Him because we love Him.

Faith beholds our Jesus ascending up on high. God is gone up with a shout, the LORD with the sound of a trumpet. Faith sees heaven's gate thrown open, the everlasting doors give way; and that very Jesus, who suffered, bled, and died on Calvary's tree the accursed death of the cross, now rising up to glory as Head over all things to His body the church, and sitting down at the right hand of the Majesty in the heavens as Lord of all. Faith delights to see it, and to crown Him Lord of all! O how blessed it is to have faith's view of a precious Christ! To see Him in His covenant engagements; to follow Him in His incarnation, life, obedience, sufferings, death, and resurrection;

and then to follow Him in His ascension to glory, and to behold Him for ever living there carrying on the cause of His church and people.

God Almighty bless the feeble efforts made to set forth a precious Jesus. The happiest moments I have is in lifting up Jesus on the pole of the everlasting gospel; in exalting, extolling, and setting Him up on high as the all in all in the salvation of His people. It is now more than twenty years ago since the Lord Jesus Christ, my sovereign Lord and Master, employed me in this blessed work of lifting up the stem of Jesse's rod, and crowning Him Lord of all. I can say it to His praise and honour, the longer I serve Him, the more I love Him, and desire to spend and be spent in His service. Well might Dr. Watts say,

> Join all the glorious names
>   Of wisdom, love, and power,
> That ever mortals knew,
>   That ever angels bore;
> All are too mean to speak his worth,
>   Too mean to set my Saviour forth.

The preciousness, the majesty, and the glory of our Lord and Master can never be told. His blessedness can never be fully described or known, till we wake up in His likeness, and see Him as He is!

8

God The Helper

PREACHED AT ZOAR CHAPEL, GREAT ALIE STREET, LONDON,
ON THURSDAY EVENING, NOVEMBER 17, 1842

*"For he hath said, I will never leave thee, nor forsake thee; so
that we may boldly say, the Lord is my helper, and I will not
fear what man shall do unto me." (Heb. 13. 5, 6.)*

The apostle Peter, speaking in reference to the Lord and His
promises, has this blessed mode of expression, "whereby are
given unto us exceeding great and precious promises."
Beloved, the exceeding greatness and preciousness of the
promises that God has made to His people are inseparably
connected with two things. The first is, that they must be
brought in their experience into those circumstances that God
has promised, for it is impossible that any one of His family can
enjoy the exceeding greatness and preciousness of these
promises unless they stand in need of what He has promised.
The other thing is that though we have the promises in the
letter of God's word, in great and rich abundance, and given by
the Lord as a revelation of His mind and will, yet you and I
cannot enjoy the fulness and preciousness thereof, unless God
applies them by the influences of His Spirit to our soul.
Have you never been in peculiar troubles, with deep
exercises of mind, and many difficulties surrounding you,
which your heavenly Father in His godly wisdom has seen fit to
exercise you with; and in your trouble you have gone to the

Bible, which is very proper, and have searched the scriptures for some promise to reach your case, and afford some consolation to your drooping mind, and could not get one? And thus, while you have seen there was an adaptation to your state and circumstances in the letter of the promise, yet, until the Holy Spirit shone upon the word, and applied it with power to your soul, you could not get at an experimental enjoyment of it? So we find we stand in need of God to give us the promises by the bedewings of His blessed Spirit. Now I know some talk as though the christian could lay hold of the promise and act faith and enjoy the God of the promise, just as he pleases. Such professors of religion know nothing of the grace and preciousness of the promise, in a way of real experience!

Notice that Paul knew the truth of what he said in the text, "I will never leave thee, nor forsake thee." You recollect that he had had a thorn in the flesh, the messenger of Satan to buffet him. He was sorely tried and harrassed, and his flesh and blood did not like it. He murmured and repined against it, and prayed earnestly that it might be taken away: but it was not the will of the Lord to remove this trouble; the thorn in the flesh must continue; he must have it, lest he should be exalted above measure, and to keep him down in his proper place.

Our flesh and blood do not like troubles; and when temptations, persecutions, afflictions, and chastisements arise, they are not pleasant, but very grievous to us; yet God's children must have troubles and crosses, for the trial of their faith, and the exercise of their patience, that they may be kept humble and in their proper place. If it were not for these things, we should not call upon the Lord to support us, to help us, to preserve us, and to guide and lead us. Suppose we had no troubles or trials, what would be the result? Why, we should rest upon our lees, and be satisfied with the things of time and sense. But when we are brought into deep waters, and into the furnace of affliction — what is the result then? Why we are made to cry unto the Lord from a feeling of deep necessity, and He encourages us with such a promise as this, "Call upon me in the day of trouble; I will deliver thee, and thou shalt glorify me."

I can speak on this subject from experience, and say in the presence of the Lord and you tonight, that I have gone hundreds of times into my closet, and fallen on my knees, which I never should have done if it had not been for the troubles, trials, and difficulties that laid in my way. What a mercy it is that the God of heaven and earth is our heavenly Father! and that we are privileged to go and tell Him all our troubles and sorrows; that He is a Father that loves us at all times; and One to whom we may tell all our secrets, who never has nor ever will betray us at any time, but who encourages us to draw near to the throne of His grace with a true heart in the confidence of faith, to commit our way to Him, and to repose upon His faithfulness and love. However thorny may be your path and whatever difficulties you may have to contend with, if through them the Lord indulges you with nearness to Himself, your troubles and sorrows will then become real blessings to you. How my soul longs for more of this sweet familiarity and blessed access to the Lord! to have more implicit trust and confidence in Him! and to enjoy more of the smiles and approbation of the Lord! When He brings us to His feet in this way, who then can give us trouble? When He is graciously pleased to pour in a little of His oil and wine, then the child of God can say in the words of the text, and bless Him for an experience of it, "the Lord is my helper, and I will not fear what man can do unto me." Yes at such a time as this he can boldly say, 'Lord, thou art my helper!'

There are three things contained in the text, which I shall enlarge upon as the Lord may be graciously pleased to assist.

First, — That the Lord has said, He will never leave nor forsake His people.

Secondly. — That the enjoyment of the promise emboldens the christian to say, that the Lord is his helper.

Thirdly. — That when realizing these things, the christian can boldly say that he will not fear what man can do unto him.

Now I know that I may speak to you of the promises, and of the things connected with them, in a consistent and systematic way, and all be God's truth; and you may sit and hear, and approve of it in your judgment, and be satisfied from the bottom of your hearts that it is according to the truth; but yet, after all, unless it is accompanied by the sweet dew and influences of the Holy Spirit, it will be dry and barren both for me to speak, and also for you to hear. This is not because there is any dryness or barrenness in God's truth; it arises from you and me and shews we stand in need of His bedewing influences in our hearts, to enable us so to receive the truth as to comfort, revive, and animate our souls. O then, Thou great Head of Thy church! grant that we may have a little heavenly dew, and some sweet refreshings of Thy grace tonight! And, my friends, may you be helped to look through the feeble instrument to the Lord of life and power, that our meeting together may be for His glory, and for the comfort and consolation of our spirits.

The Lord has said that *He will never leave nor forsake His people.*

First, let us enquire who is intended by the pronoun "He" in the text, who, it is said, "will never leave nor forsake His people. It is no less a person than the Lord of hosts Himself. It is the Creator of heaven and earth. It is our covenant God and Father in the Lord Jesus Christ who has solemnly declared that He made a covenant with His chosen, and sworn unto David His servant, that his seed shall be established for ever, and his throne to all generations; and that "one generation shall praise his works to another, and shall declare his mighty acts." All the purposes and decrees of a covenant God stand as firm as Jehovah's throne. "Hath he said it; and will he not do it? Hath he spoken it; and shall it not come to pass?" Yea, it shall stand fast for ever! "Heaven and earth shall pass away, but my words shall not pass away." "He is faithful that hath promised;" and He never can nor ever will deny Himself. "If we believe not, yet he abideth faithful; he cannot deny himself." God's faithfulness stands firm and sure. What an unspeakable blessing it is that we have a faithful covenant-keeping God to rely upon! His people have had to say of Him in all ages of the world, that not one thing has failed of all that He has spoken; for He has always been faithful to His word of promise. "I will never leave thee, nor forsake thee." What He says, He does.

In the next place, let us notice *the persons to whom the Lord has spoken this promise,* "I will never leave thee, nor forsake thee." These words have reference to what the Lord said to Jacob from the top of the ladder. Jacob was in sore trouble; he had left his native home, and was fleeing into a distant land for his life; his brother Esau was determined to be revenged upon him because he had obtained the blessing: and Jacob, being wearied with his journey, had laid himself down on the ground; a stone was his pillow, and the canopy of heaven was his covering; and he was looking to the Lord for protection. Now here was Jacob in this forlorn condition; and he had fallen asleep, when the Lord, who was watching over him, appeared to him in a vision of the night, at the top of the ladder; and which was a type of Christ, in whom every promise that God has made is deposited, "for all the promises of God in him are yea, and in him amen, unto the glory of God by us." From the top of this ladder the Lord said to Jacob, "Behold, I am with thee, and will keep thee; and I will not leave thee until I have done that which I have spoken to thee of." This promise was spoken home to his heart; it was attended with the gracious bedewings and sacred influences of the Lord, who declared Himself to be his covenant God and Father, as He had also been the God of Abraham, and the God of his father Isaac. Jacob was so overpowered with the revelation, and felt the blessedness of it in such a way, that he said, "This is none other but the house of God, and this is the gate of heaven!" Here then, God made a glorious promise to Jacob. The prophet Isaiah has a peculiar reference to it, where he says, "Fear not, thou worm Jacob, and ye men of Israel! I will help thee, saith the LORD, and thy Redeemer, the Holy One of Israel." Jacob was typical of the whole spiritual Israel; and therefore the promise was not made to him merely, but to every one of the people of God in him.

Let us enquire, then, a little more into the character to whom the promise was made. We say it was made to Jacob. But what was Jacob? He was a poor, weak, and helpless worm; and God knew that he felt himself to be sinful and wretched; and therefore He says, "Fear not, thou worm Jacob." If you do not see and feel yourselves to be poor, weak, lost, and helpless worms; and are not brought to know it as Jacob did, the promise is not made to you. To every one that knows himself to be in such a condition, and can feelingly say, 'I am a worm, and no man; I am a poor, weak, and worthless worm!' God says, "I will never leave thee." Bless the Lord, then, that He notices such wretched and such creeping worms as we discover ourselves to be in our feelings.

But again, to whom does the Lord speak this promise? It is to *those who have many fears,* and are sorely troubled and distressed in heart on account of what they have to pass through. This was the case with Jacob. He had sore trials and discouragements; and he feared that he should fall, and not be able to stand his ground, so that his mind was greatly cast down. This will always be the case in the time of trouble and great affliction; and therefore the Lord encourages him, and speaks comfortably to his heart, and says, "Fear not, thou worm Jacob; for I am with thee; be not dismayed, for I am thy God; I will strengthen thee, yea, I will help thee, yea, I will uphold thee with the right hand of my righteousness." Are you ever dismayed and cast down, and tossed to and fro in your feelings; and made to wonder at times where the scene will end? If so, you are the characters intended, and it is to such as you to whom the promise is made; for the Lord's people are the subjects of many fears. There are a great many "fear-nots" in the scriptures but not one too many, or else the Lord would not have scattered them up and down in the word of His grace as He has done. He has not spoken them that the children of God may be nursed up in doubts and fears, but that their hearts may be encouraged to trust in the Lord, and their minds established in the faithfulness of His truth.

But again. "He hath said, I will never leave thee, nor forsake thee." To whom then has He said it? It is to *those who feel that they are not worthy of* being the recipients of such a glorious truth. If a man or woman present here tonight should think they are worthy of this blessing, it is evident that they are not interested in the promise. I cannot but admire the riches of God's grace to such poor worthless characters, as the people of God see and feel themselves to be. John the Baptist felt himself to be so insignificant, that he said, "the latchet of his shoes I am not worthy to unloose"! The Centurion said, "I am not worthy that thou shouldest enter into my house". The believing family know that they are not worthy of such rich promises, and of such wonderful dealings of loving-kindness and faithfulness. How do we feel when we approach the Maker of heaven and earth? Can we tell Him that we are worthy of His notice, of His help, of His comfort, and of His consolations? Oh no! The heaven-born soul, made acquainted with himself, has no patience with anything of the kind. He says, "I am worthless! I am astonished that the Lord exercises so much patience and long-suffering in bearing with me; for I am sure, if He were to mark my iniquities, and to deal with me according to my deserts, He would cut me down as a cumberer of the ground!" Such an one is satisfied, not on account of any worthiness in him, but because God will bless His people, and stand by the faithfulness of His promise. He hath said, who cannot lie, "I will never leave thee, nor forsake thee."

Let us glance at two or three other promises. Depend upon it, there shall be a fulfilment of them in our experience, let our circumstances be whatever they may. When speaking to His fearing and cast-down people, the Lord says, "Fear not, for I have redeemed thee: when thou passest through the waters, I will be with thee; and through the rivers, they shall not overflow thee: when thou walkest through the fire, thou shalt not be burned; neither shall the flame kindle upon thee." So we must go through the waters and the fires; and the Lord will make good His promise to us in them: He will be with us in trouble; He will never leave us in the waters or the flames. Bless Him, then, for His promise!

Look now at the children of Israel, when they were in captivity in Egypt, did the Lord forget them there? No; for when the time was accomplished to deliver them, He brought them out with an high hand and an out-stretched arm; and they passed through the sea as on dry land, for God was with them. When the three Hebrew children were cast into the fiery furnace, the Lord of hosts was with them. He always fulfils this promise in their experience, "I will never leave thee, nor forsake thee." He will be with them in all their sorrows, troubles, and afflictions. Whatever floods and flames we may have to go through, the Lord will be with us; He will never leave us. It is all right then, He is on our side; and greater is He that is for us, than all that can be opposed to us.

Let us look at another promise. The Lord says, "I will bring the blind by a way that they knew not; I will lead them in paths that they have not known: I will make darkness light before them, and crooked things straight. These things will I do unto them, and not forsake them." I see somewhat in these sweet words, which I hope will meet your case and comfort your souls. "I will lead the blind by a way that they knew not." This does not mean those that are blind literally, but those of the Lord's own covenant people, who are hedged up in their way, and cannot understand His dealings with them in a way of

providence and grace. Have I here tonight one of these characters, who is thus wound up in his feelings and circumstances,
and knows not what to do? Let me tell you, the Lord will
surely take you by the hand, and lead aright, for He says, He
will never leave thee, nor forsake thee. I read of one of the
family, who said, "I will lift up mine eyes unto the hills from
whence cometh my help; my help cometh from the Lord, which
made heaven and earth." It is He who "will lead the blind by a
way that they knew not."

We very frequently cannot understand our path, or know the
way in which we are being led; but the Lord has given us His
faithful promise, and says, "I will make darkness light before
thee, and crooked things straight." Have you any darkness in
your soul; do you feel oppositions arising to every inch of the
way, and do many doubts and fears spring up in consequence?
This is the way that all the saints of God have had to travel
through the wilderness. The Psalmist says of those who are
unacquainted with these things, "because they have no changes,
therefore they fear not God." The wicked are without changes,
there is no fear of God before their eyes, so that "they are not
in trouble as other men, neither are they plagued like other
men." But the people of God have their times of darkness and
desertion with many misgivings and fears; and if it were not so,
the promise would not be suitable to them. Should there be
anyone present in these circumstances, the language of the text
belongs to you, "he will never leave thee, nor forsake thee."
"Who is among you that feareth the Lord, that obeyeth the
voice of his servant, that walketh in darkness, and hath no
light? let him trust in the name of the LORD, and stay upon his
God;" for He is a faithful God. What a mercy it is, that we have
such a covenant keeping God to stay upon. What a foundation
is this for the fulfilment of the promise!

Again, "He will make crooked things straight." Have you
not some crooked things? Is all straight at home, and just as
you would have it to be? Is there no husband got a crooked
wife — or wife troubled with a bad husband? Are there no
difficulties in the business, or disorders in the family, or
crookedness in the circumstances? Is all right and straight? If
so, the promise does not belong to you, it is only intended for
those who are walking in these crooked places. 'Well then,' says
some poor soul, 'that just suits me, for I have nothing but cares,

sorrows, and crosses, and though I try to make things straight, I cannot do it, for the more I strive, the more crooked they appear. Such will cry out in earnest supplication, 'O that the Lord would look upon me, and make the crooked things in my path straight, and the rough places plain!' May the Lord enable you to leave your case with Him; for He is faithful, and He will fulfil His promise. After you have tried to alter the crooks in your lot and mend matters, you have discovered that you have made them much worse than they were before: and when you have been thoroughly taught your own helplessness, then the Lord will come and make good His own promise; "He will make crooked things straight, and rough places plain; and all these things will he do, and not forsake them."

We used to have a very valuable old man in Lancashire, who for more than half a century had exhibited a most exemplary character; and there was a young man with whom he was very familiar who had left that part of the country and had gone into the ministry. Many months rolled away since they had seen each other, but having occasion to travel to a place some distance from their homes, they met most unexpectedly together at the end of their journey, when, after a good hearty shake of the hand, and saying how glad they were to meet again, the young man said, 'Well, Richard, how are you getting on?' The old man made answer, 'Do you mean respecting my farm, or my family?' 'No,' he replied, 'I want to know how you are getting on in your conscience?' 'Why,' he says, 'the Lord and me have not been friends for some time; for I had been pleading and wrestling with Him to deliver me from a particular trouble that pressed heavily upon me; and though I had told Him all about it, yet He appeared to take no notice of me; and the burden that I wanted to be removed got heavier and heavier, until at last it was almost insupportable. Then I became peevish, fretful, and rebellious as Jonah was, so that things got worse and worse in my soul.' The young man said, 'But you are something better now?' 'O yes,' he replied, 'because I have been able since then to give it all up into His hands; for I said, 'Lord, I give it all up to Thee; do with me as Thou wilt; and make me to be resigned to Thy will:' and blessings on His name, I have found Him to be my covenant God and Father, and faithful to His word of promise, so that all is right and straight again.'

Just so it is, when we are brought to submit to His will, and are made able to leave all to His management, then it is that we prove Him to be a faithful covenant-keeping God, who will fulfil His promises to His saints, and surely do them good, because it has pleased Him to make them His people. He knows all their wants and necessities, and He will satisfy them all out of His riches in glory by Christ Jesus. If we could leave our cares more in the hands of our God, and cast our burdens more upon Him who cares for us, we should have more repose and quietness in our souls. But you and I are unable to do this; for we can no more cast our cares upon Him in our own strength, than we can make a world! It is only as the Lord enables us to roll our troubles on Him, and leave them in His blessed hands, that we can do it at all. When we are thus privileged, we feel the sweetness of it, and learn experimentally the faithfulness of His promise, "I will never leave thee, nor forsake thee."

II.   We move on now, to the second branch of the subject — that *the enjoyment of the promise emboldens the believer to say, "the Lord is my helper."* Having proved the Lord to be faithful to His word, and of His raising up faithful living witnesses to testify to the faithfulness of God to His promise, we take encouragement therefrom and boldly say, that He who has helped us thus far, will never leave us now, but He will be with us through all the way, and guide us by His counsel, and afterward receive us to His glory. "So that we may boldly say, the Lord is my helper, and I will not fear what man can do unto me."

In reference to the help of the Lord, then, there are a few things which it is necessary for us to notice. How many of us are there, who feelingly know that we need the Lord to help us, through a discovery of our utter helplessness and misery? Until we are brought into an acquaintance with this solemn truth, we shall never feel our want of divine help.

In the first place, we need *the saving help* of the Lord. "O Israel," He says, "thou hast destroyed thyself, but in me is thy help found." We have no help in us, for "vain is the help of man." We are lost and ruined by nature — sunk in sin, guilt, and misery — condemned, and under the curse of the law; and not the angels in heaven, nor all the ministers on earth, can help a sinner out of the rubbish of the fall, nor help him to the salvation which is in Christ. There is a good deal said by some persons about man's power and ability to help himself, and that he might do a great deal if he would; but, my friends, we know by experience that we had no power to help ourselves. We were dead in sin, and lay at the very dark door of hell; and had it not been for the interposition of the Lord Jesus Christ, the immortal Word, taking our cause into His hands by becoming incarnate, standing in our law-place and stead, and overwhelmed in sorrows and sufferings to raise us up from our miserable state in the ruins of the fall, not a soul of us could ever have been saved! I cannot but admire that sweet passage of David, and it has done my soul good many times, both in private and public, where he says, that "help is laid on one mighty to save!" Here we might say many things on the ability of the Lord Jesus Christ, and shew that "he is able to save unto the uttermost all that come unto God by him."

We need the help of the Lord *all through the wilderness.* We need His help to enable us to keep constant and faithful to the profession of His truth, therefore the apostle says "stand fast, quit you like men." This is a day of awful departure from the truth of God; and it is lamentable to see how some ministers are swerving and sliding back from that which they once professed, turning aside into error, and causing the Philistines to rejoice. May the Lord help us to stand fast, and never to give up that truth which debases the sinner in the dust and puts the crown on the head of the Lord Jesus Christ. The Lord help you to plead with His blessed Majesty not to allow you either to court the smiles, nor fear the frowns of any man; but to be kept faithful and honest in the conscience; to be girt about with the whole armour of truth; and to be able to wield the sword of the Spirit, in dependence upon His promised aid; and to leave all consequences in the hands of the Lord and Master. The Lord helps not only His people, but His ministers also, that they be made valiant for the truth; and when at any time they may appear to slacken, may you be enabled to pray for them, and to encourage them in their work. Thus, Lord, grant that the purity of Thy truth may continue among us!

The apostle Paul prophesied that "the time will come when they will not endure sound doctrine; but after their own lusts shall they heap to themselves teachers, having itching ears; and they shall turn away their ears from the truth, and shall be turned unto fables." The time is come now. For do we not now see great numbers admitted into the churches who have never been brought out of the world, and who are destitute of any experimental knowledge of the truth as it is in Jesus; so that the Lord is not known, nor His precious discriminating truth loved? Where this is the case, such hearers cannot endure sound doctrine nor genuine christian experience; but they must have teachers, who will amuse their fancies, and play upon their passions, to the neglecting of the pure truth of God. But nevertheless, the Lord is the helper of His true spiritual Zion; for He promised never to leave His Zion, but He will be with her, and bless her. The Lord is the best helper of his people!

But I observe again, we need the Lord's help *to enable us to stand fast* in an open profession of attachment to Christ's person, His word, and His people. There are many sufferings we are called to endure. I have had so many things to contend with that my flesh has been ready to give it all up many times; and if I could have run away from the work I should have done it, though I speak it to my shame and disgrace. I have often said, "Would to God I had never entered into the work of the ministry at all." But the Lord does enable His people to stand; We need the Lord, then, to be our helper and sustainer, that we may continue faithful to Him and His work, and to be "instant in season and out of season."

We need the Lord to direct and guide us in every step we take. I am jealous over my heart, and my carnal reasonings; they bring me many times upon my knees before the Lord, to pray Him to keep me in my right mind, that He would be a strength to me, and guide me in the way in which He would have me to go. He has promised to hold His people up; and I am a living witness to the faithfulness of that God who has held me up now for many years. Therefore I can say with beloved Paul, "having obtained help of God I continue unto this day"! I love this solemn saying of his in my very heart and soul: for if God had not held Paul up through his multiplied troubles, he must have fainted; but the Lord supported him, and brought him through all his difficulties. He had to suffer many things from false brethren; some left him, and went into crooked paths; others departed into the world, and turned their backs on him; while at one important time, he says, "no man stood with me, but all men forsook me; nevertheless the Lord stood with me, and strengthened me." Many failed him, but his God never forsook him; He stood by and supported him, and made him triumphant over all his enemies. The Lord will help His people to the end. How often is the soul enabled to erect an Ebenezer of praise and gratitude to Him and say, "Lord, hitherto hast thou helped me"!

Now we have abundant proof from the word of truth that God will never leave His people. Did He forsake the Prophet in the wilderness? Did He not send ravens night and morning, with bread, to sustain him? Did He forsake the poor widow woman of Sarepta? Did not the barrel of meal last, and the cruse of oil continue to flow, until the time came that there was plenty in the land? Did He forsake Daniel in the den of lions? Or, can it be proved that He has ever forsaken one of His saints? No; "there is not one good thing failed of all that the Lord hath spoken."

Then again, the help of the Lord appears *in raising up the soul from bondage* and misery, and bringing it into an experimental enjoyment of gospel liberty. During the time the preciousness of the truth is being opened up to the mind, there will be a sweet peace felt in the Lord, and a reposing upon Him; for "thou wilt keep in perfect peace, whose mind is stayed on thee; because he trusteth in thee."

III.   We come to the third and last part of the text. *The experience of these things in the soul enables the believer to say, that he will "not fear what man can do unto him."* No man can do anything against one of God's saints, but what He is pleased to permit him to do. The Master Himself said to Pilate, "thou couldest have no power at all against me, except it were given thee from above." And so it is, that neither men nor devils nor any other power, unless God gives permission, can touch one of His anointed. The Lord says to the angry passions of man, and the rage of devils, as He does to the winds and the waves, "hitherto shalt thou go, and no further; and here shall thy proud waves be stayed." We need not fear what man shall do unto us; for he shall not do anything but what the Lord has appointed, and which He will overrule for His own glory, and for the good of His dear people. He encourages us not to be afraid of the fury of man, saying, "Fear not them which can kill the body, and after that have no more which they can do."

Were not the minds of the martyrs raised up above the sufferings of their bodies? Did not our fore-fathers that suffered at the stake in Smithfield and on Tower Hill, die triumphantly, resigning their souls into the Lord's hands, in the full confidence of faith? Were not these martyrs raised up above the fear of man, beyond their agonies, and died sealing the truth in their blood? May we not then boldly say, " we will not fear what man can do unto us?" The religion of Jesus will raise the mind above the fear of man!

Look at the case of the three Hebrew children, Shadrach, Meshach, and Abednego, and see how they were carried above the fear of man. The idolatrous king, Nebuchadnezzar, had erected a golden image, and issued a proclamation that at certain times all men should bow down to it: but these servants of the living God were determined not to worship the idol which the king had caused to be made, nor did they make a secret of their intention not to obey His command. They are watched, and speedily brought before the king, and accused of disobedience to his will. The anger of the monarch rises like the fury of a lion; and he says to them, 'Is it true, what I hear of thee, that you refuse to fall down and worship the image which I have made; and have I not decreed that such shall be cast into the midst of a burning fiery furnace?' They answered the king, and said, 'It is true, O king; and we are not careful to answer thee in this matter; for be it known unto thee, that we will not serve thy gods, nor worship the golden image which thou hast made!' Then the king, full of fury, with his countenance distorted with rage, commanded the furnace to be heated seven times more than usual, and these servants of the most high God to be thrown into the midst of it, saying 'And where is that God that can deliver out of my hands?' O what impiety and blasphemy! They replied, 'Why, that God, whom we fear and love, and in whom we put our trust, He is able to deliver us from the burning fiery furnace; and He will deliver us out of thy hands. O king! we have put our case into His hands, and know that He will never leave us nor forsake us!' And now, behold them in the fire. Has the Lord forsaken them? No, He is with them still! He is walking with them in the midst of the fire. Then the king, expecting to have seen them consumed in a moment, turned to his counsellors in great astonishment, and said, "Did not we cast three men bound into the midst of the fire and behold, I see four men loose, walking in the midst of the fire, and they have no hurt; and the form of the fourth is like unto the Son of God." Yes; the Captain of the Lord's host had come down, and was present with His saints, and by His mighty power had changed the nature of the fiery flames, so that they received no injury therefrom. Thus they triumphed over the fury of the king, and were not afraid what man could do unto them. "If God be for us, who can be against us?"

The power of the Lord in raising the mind above the fear of man, may be seen in the case of *Elisha's servant.* When he had arisen early in the morning and got up on the mountain, he returned with great haste full of fears exclaiming, 'Alas! my master, how shall we do!' as though he had said, 'it is all up with us now;' for he perceived the host that encompassed the city around both with horses and chariots, and he concluded it was all over with them. But the Prophet was not alarmed; he was quiet and composed; and said "Fear not, for they that be with us are more than they that be with them." He knew that the Omnipotent God was with him; and that the Lord of hosts was on his side. But the servant of the man of God could not conceive who was with him; and he says, 'Master, they are now surrounding the city like unto grasshoppers to take us!' Then the Prophet prayed the Lord to open the eyes of the young man, that he might see how they were secured, and he beheld the mountain surrounded with horses and chariots of fire for their protection. He saw then, that there were more for them than all the hosts of the Syrians that were assembled against them; and he was satisfied, and no longer feared what man could do unto them.

O that the Lord would raise up our minds more above ourselves and our fellow-creatures and enable us to leave our cares in His hands; to trust in Him, to look more unto Him, and to rest on His faithful promise, "I will never leave thee, nor forsake thee; so that we may boldly say, The Lord is my helper, and I will not fear what man shall do unto me."

May the Lord add His blessing to what has been said, and His name shall have the praise. Amen.

9

Immutability

PREACHED AT ZOAR CHAPEL, GREAT ALIE STREET, LONDON
ON THURSDAY EVENING, MAY 26, 1853.

"Jesus Christ the same yesterday, and to-day, and for ever."
(Hebrews 18. 8.)

What a mercy, my hearers, that our Jesus, on whom we build
our souls' eternal all, is "the same yesterday, and to-day, and
for ever"! Whatever we look at, save the God of our salvation,
we see changing. Look at the world and the things of the world
— its fashion is changed. The Psalmist David had his mind
awed with a view of the world, as we find in the concluding
part of Ps. 102; and Paul brings David's language forward in
Hebrews 1, showing that all things are fleeting, but the Lord is
unchangeable. "He weakened my strength in the way; he
shortened my days. I said, O my God, take me not away in the
midst of my days; thy years are throughout all generations. Of
old hast thou laid the foundation of the earth; and the heavens
are the work of thy hands. They shall perish, but thou shalt
endure; yea, all of them shall wax old like a garment; as a
vesture shalt thou change them, and they shall be changed; but
thou art the same, and thy years shall have no end." (Ps. 102.
23-27.) Our Jesus was in the beginning the Creator of the

heavens and the earth, and all that therein is; our Jesus is the same Almighty God today, and He will be the same tomorrow and for ever. O what a mercy that our Jesus, the God of our salvation, is so unalterable, so eternally immutable!

Again, on the negative side of the question: if we look at nations, and empires, and monarchs, they rise and fall; but there is no alteration in our Jesus. Hear His voice: "By me kings reign and princes decree justice;" He upholds one and puts down another at His sovereign pleasure. God's ministers are to exalt Him: "Say unto Zion, Thy God reigneth" as the God of nations, and will cause all things to work together for His honour and the good of His chosen family.

Further, if we look at families, what changes there are in them! Where are our fathers? do they live for ever? No; one generation goes, another comes. But not so with our Jesus: "I am he that liveth, and was dead; and, behold, I am alive for evermore."

Look at churches; what changes take place in them! Ministers that have stood on Zion's walls and blown the silver trumpet of the everlasting gospel are removed. They are the subject of mortality, like the high priest under the law; and the loss is frequently greatly felt. But our Jesus, the great Shepherd and Bishop of souls, will never die; He is "the same yesterday, and to-day, and for ever;" and the church is as near and dear to Him as ever it was. But as we see the Lord's servants removed from the sphere of usefulness into the immediate presence of the divine Master, we are to "pray. . . the Lord of the harvest that he would send forth labourers into his harvest." The residue of the Spirit is with Him.

Look at members of Christian churches; do they continue? No. How many that have worshipped God in this place, that have stood in church fellowship with God's Zion here, have been removed from the church militant to the church triumphant in glory. But our Jesus still lives; He still remains; He was "the same yesterday," and He is the same "to-day," and He will be the same "for ever." We sometimes greatly feel the loss of our brethren and sisters in the Lord, with whom we have taken sweet counsel, and walked in peace and soul-union in the house of God; when death has overtaken them we have sorrowed, but our sorrow has not been as those that have no hope. I have abundant reason to feel in this sense, as the pastor of a Christian church. In the midst of bereavements of this description, we have this consolation, that whatever the Lord takes away from the church on earth to the church in heaven, He never takes away Himself. O no! Jesus is here still: "Jesus Christ the same yesterday," that dwelt in the church in the wilderness in the prophetic dispensation, in the days of the apostles, in the days of our persecuted fathers the Puritans, that dwells in the church "to-day," and will still dwell in it when we are dead and gone. "Jesus Christ the same yesterday, and to-day, and for ever." One text in particular has greatly soothed my sorrows arising from bereavements in the loss of near and dear friends, is where the Psalmist David says, "The Lord liveth; and blessed be my rock; and let the God of my salvation be exalted," He ever did live; He lives now; He lives in the hearts of His people; He lives in Zion; and He will be there tomorrow, and the next day, and for ever. O the immutability, the constancy, and firmness of the dear Redeemer!

We observe again, that sometimes there are many changes in our own minds. We are the subjects of change and mutability. What is more fickle than we are? Sometimes we are on the mount of enjoyment: "Bless the Lord, O my soul;" sometimes we are in unbelief and temptation: "Is his mercy clean gone for ever?" Jesus lives, whatever be the state of our minds. Sometimes we are walking in darkness, under the hidings of our heavenly Father's face; sometimes we have the liftings up of the light of His countenance; but Jesus lives when we are in the dark as well as when we are in the light. There is no alienation nor the least shadow of a turn with our blessed Jesus.

The Lord enable us to make a few remarks upon Jesus, "the same yesterday, and to-day, and for ever."

I. In the first place, we may look at the Lord Jesus Christ *in the love of His heart.* We pause upon that; it is a pleasing subject for us to look at; the love of His heart, His fond affections, firmly fixed upon the objects of His eternal choice from before all worlds. The concluding part of that memorable chapter, Proverbs 8, abundantly proves that His delight was with them before any part of creation was begun. Christ loved His people from the beginning with an everlasting love; as the effect of that love, He became their covenant Head, their Surety, and Mediator. It was the love of His heart that constrained him to "throw His radiant glory by," and veil His Godhead in a clay tabernacle; that constrained Him to suffer, bleed, and die, "the just for the unjust." "Herein is love, not that we loved God, but that God loved us," and that "when we were enemies," as the effect of that love, "Christ died for us." And having finished and completed salvation's work in fulfilment of His covenant engagement He has entered into heaven itself, and is the church's Head and representative in glory; with the love of His heart firmly fixed on His church to this day; and, blessed be His name, He does not love His church in glory one jot or tittle more than His church on earth. The church in glory is more happy and blessed, but not more near and dear to the Redeemer, not more locked up in His heart, than His spouse, His bride, in this her militant state of trial and difficulty on earth. Neither our corruption inwardly, nor our sins outwardly, nor the powers of darkness unitedly, can ever turn the loving heart of Jesus away from His people. It is always the same. Hearken to the solemn declaration; there is food in it for our souls: Jesus "having loved his own which were in the world, he loved them unto the end." His love does not, cannot change as ours does.

In His love to His people, our Lord Jesus Christ "sticketh closer than a brother." Amongst brethren there is sometimes love, and a very blessed and comfortable thing it is to walk in the fear of the Lord, and the unity of the Spirit, and in the bond of peace; but Satan makes inroads, our evil hearts are stirred up, and there is "a crook in the lot," something of a perplexing and trying nature, and our love one to another begins to wax cold, and sometimes angry words ensue; and when this is the case it is very painful. Paul and Barnabas were two of the most blessed men of God that ever had an existence as Christians and as ministers; and yet they strove together about taking Mark with them, and the contention between those good men was so sharp that they parted one from another. When we take one view of the matter, we are ready to say, "What a pity that those two good men should thus fall out by the way and separate." But take another view of the subject; Paul says it turned out for the furtherance of the gospel. The Lord overruled it for good; Paul went one way and Barnabas another, and they preached the glad tidings of the gospel, and thus the Redeemer's kingdom was spread. But, Jesus' loving heart never altered to either of them. His love is fixed upon His church in all her trials and in all her difficulties. He is "Jesus Christ the same yesterday, and to-day, and for ever."

We should take into consideration, that the eye of Jesus Christ our King, Lord, and Law-giver, is ever upon us. He has given us many precepts and exhortations in His word; it is for His honour that we walk in them; it is for our comfort and consolation that we obey them. "In keeping his commandments there is great reward;" but if we disobey the directions our blessed Lord and Master has given us, He "will visit our iniquity with a rod, and our transgressions with stripes." This He does in love, for His lovingkindness will He not take away from us, nor suffer His faithfulness to fail. Zion once thought that the Lord had forgotten her, and that He ceased to love her, and had forsaken her. She said, "The Lord hath forsaken me, and my God hath forgotten me." "Ah!" says the devil, "and he will never be favourable to thee any more; he will never look upon thee in love and mercy, nor visit thee again!" It is a lie; and the devil was a liar from the beginning. What says our Lord? "Can a woman forget her sucking child, that she should not have compassion on the son of her womb?" I have known mothers turn their backs even upon their infants; but the Lord Jesus says, "I will not forget thee." "I have graven thee upon the palms of my hands; thy walls are continually before me;" and "I will not forget thee."

What a mercy that our Lord Jesus is "the same yesterday, and to-day, and for ever!" He does not love His people's sins, nor their failings, nor their infirmities; He did not love Peter's denial of Him with oaths and curses; He did not love David's fall, for "the thing that he did displeased him;" but He loves His children, and will never leave them nor forsake them. Paul exulted in this: "Who shall separate us from the love of Christ? Shall tribulation, or distress, or persecution, or famine, or nakedness, or peril, or sword?" Shall any or all of these things combined dissolve the union that exists between Christ and His church? No; it is an indissoluble union; for "we are more than conquerors, through him that loved us." O what a blessing that Jesus Christ is the same! "I am the LORD, I change not; therefore ye sons of Jacob are not consumed." If our Jesus were not immutable, we could not stand; it is of the Lord's mercies that we are not consumed. The mercy of the Lord is like Jesus, "from everlasting to everlasting;" The mercy of the LORD endureth for ever." So that the loving heart of the Lord Jesus Christ is ever firmly fixed upon His spouse; and He is the same in His regard for her "yesterday, and to-day, and for

ever." He "rests in his love." The Lord enable us to rest where
He rests.

Young Christians are very prone to judge of their state
according to the frame of their mind. When they are very
happy and comfortable, and enjoying the sweet love of Christ
in their souls, they say, "I am a child of God, I love the Lord,
and all is right." When the Lord withdraws the light of His
countenance, and they have no sweet feeling of the love of
Christ in their souls, but have hard, cold, and barren hearts, a
backwardness to do what is good and a forwardness to do what
is evil, Satan assails them at every point, inbred corruption stirs
up, "the flesh lusting against the spirit," and misery and
wretchedness is felt in their soul. Then Satan takes advantage
and says, "The Lord does not love thee, and thou dost not love
him;" and thus the mind of the young Christian is shaken,
because he judges his state according to the feelings of his own
mind. But that is not wise judgment. "Who is there among you
that feareth the LORD, that obeyeth the voice of his servant,
that walketh in darkness, and hath no light? Let him trust in
the name of the LORD" — in the name of the Lord Jesus, "the
same yesterday, and to-day, and for ever" — "and stay himself
upon his God;" for Jesus is his God, and will ever remain so.

Heaviness may "endure for a night, but joy cometh in the
morning." Job was well instructed, but look at the argument
that he raised when he was in darkness and could not find the
Lord, though he sought Him on the right hand and on the left,
behind and before, but felt himself in a very wretched state of
soul. He said, "He knoweth the way that I take;" "I am in the
crucible; I am being tried by feeling the depravity of my nature,
the vileness of my heart; I am being tried by the temptations of
Satan; I am being tried by my friends that persecute me; and I
am being tried in God's afflicting dispensations in providence."
But see the hope, the blessed confidence at the bottom: "When
he hath tried me, I shall come forth as gold." He is Jesus still!
He will "refine them as silver is refined, and try them as gold is
tried;" and then He will say, "It is my people" after all, and will
own them still; and they shall say, "It is my God; it is my Jesus,
'the same yesterday, and to-day, and for ever.' " Bless His name
for His immutable love!

II.   But we observe, secondly, that the Lord Jesus Christ is
"the same yesterday, and to-day, and for ever," *in His power
and ability*. He possessed power and ability to create the

heavens and the earth, to speak them out of nothing into existence. He possessed power enough to bring Israel out of Egypt with a strong hand and an outstretched arm. He had power and ability to cause the Red Sea to flee before them: "The sea saw him, and fled; Jordan was driven back." He had power and ability enough to supply the wants of Israel in the wilderness; power and ability enough to bring down the walls of Jericho; power and ability enough to deliver the various idolatrous nations into their hands. In more personal circumstances, see the display of His power in the case of Daniel, and in the case of the three Hebrew children; see His power in providing for the prophet in the wilderness, in increasing the poor woman's meal, and providing for her and her son. Innumerable instances might be adduced from the book of God expressive of the greatness of the power of our blessed and glorious Lord Jesus. Now, the same Jesus that appeared as the Captain of the Lord's host upon the walls of Jericho, in the days of Joshua, is our Captain; the same blessed Son of God that appeared in Nebuchadnezzar's fiery furnace is our Jesus; and, bless His precious name, he will be the same powerful, helping Jesus to the end.

Again the Lord Jesus Christ is "the same yesterday, and to-day, and for ever," in His power, as the God of grace and salvation. I have no power in myself; I am one of those that the prophet speaks of when he says, "He giveth power to the faint; and to them that have no might he increaseth strength." I am often faint, and as weak as water; but when my blessed Jesus reveals Himself in His power, and I can claim an interest in His person, I feel my heart warm in me directly, and such texts as these have come with savour on my spirit: "All power is given to me in heaven and earth;" "Thine is the kingdom, the power, and the glory;" "They shall speak of the glory of thy kingdom, and they shall talk of thy power;" "God hath spoken once; twice have I heard this; that power belongeth unto God." It is not by creature might or power that God's cause is maintained in this sinful, crooked, and rebellious world, in spite of all opposition, but it is by the power of the Spirit of our God and of His Christ. He says, "As thou hast given him power over all flesh, that he should give eternal life to as many as thou hast given him." In allusion to this, David, in Ps. 110. 3, says, "Thy people shall be willing in the day of thy power." The power of Jesus, that brought down the lofty looks of Saul of Tarsus, has brought down thousands since. The power of Jesus that brought Zaccheus down the tree, that shook the prison and the gaoler's conscience; the power of Jesus, that arrested the dying thief on the cross; this power is still working, for He is in reference to His power, "Jesus Christ the same yesterday, and to-day, and for ever."

Let us look back for a moment. Was it our own power and ability that changed our heart, renewed our will, and turned our feet heavenward? Instead of my power and ability having anything to do with effecting it, my carnal heart fought against it. O the opposition that there is in the soul of the sinner to the work of God! But when the day of the Lord's power comes, the stoutest heart must obey, the loftiest looks must be brought down, and the Lord in His almighty power be exalted. He clothes with power the word spoken by His sent servants: "Our gospel came not unto you in word only, but also in power." Ah! we want this power. How my soul longs for power, to attend to the word preached, power to be felt in my own soul! Without this power there is nothing that will really stand the test; for religion without the power of God is but like the shadow without the substance. Religion begins with the power of God, it is maintained by the power of the Lord, and it is completed by the power of the Lord. Jesus, then, had the power in His hand "yesterday," He has the power in His hand "to-day," and He will have the power in His hand "tomorrow." When you and I are gone to heaven He will have the power still, and He will gather in the number of His elect, and bring His sons from afar and His daughters from the ends of the earth.

Further, He is "Jesus Christ, the same yesterday, and to-day, and for ever," in the power of His Spirit and grace in the souls of His people. Do we feel very weak and helpless? We are the more safe and secure. Peter did not see and feel himself so weak and helpless when he said, "Though I should die with thee, yet will I not deny thee," as Paul did when buffeted with the "thorn in the flesh," and trembling for fear of falling, and crying to the Lord to save him. The Lord keep us day by day feeling our weakness, the depravity of our nature, and the evils of our heart! Dear Lord, increase a godly jealousy in our soul; forbid that we should place any confidence and trust in ourselves, but that our confidence and trust may be in Thee and the power of Thine arm, the power of Thy Spirit and grace! The Lord is able to keep His people; they cannot keep themselves: "He that keepeth Israel neither slumbers nor sleeps." And His power is like Himself, "the same yesterday, and to-day, and for ever." These things have a very blessed place in my heart; they are very comfortable to my soul and I turn them into prayer; and when I read, "He will keep the feet of his saints," then I pray, "Do thou keep me, for I cannot keep myself; hold me up by thy power, and I shall be safe." Let the Lord be our upholder, and we are safe and secure. O that we may ever grow in confidence in the power, and ability, and all-sufficiency of Jesus Christ, and that our heart and our eyes may be daily up to Him! He is "the same yesterday, and to-day, and for ever," in His power and in His ability.

See this immutability in another respect. Are any of my brethren and sisters shut up in their souls as in a prison? God's people often know what it is, as David says, to be shut up: "I am shut up, and cannot come forth." They know what it is to sigh and groan in their prison-house. "Let the sighing and groaning of the prisoner come up before thee." Now they do not wait till they can deliver themselves. Some people talk of believing and acting faith as though it were a very easy matter; but that is not the faith that stands in God's wisdom and power. The children of God that are shut up in the feelings of their own minds could no more effect their own deliverance from bondage into the glorious liberty of the gospel than they could keep God's holy law. The Lord has reserved this power to Himself: "The spirit of the Lord GOD is upon me; because the Lord hath anointed me to preach the gospel to the poor, to set at liberty them that are bound." If we want liberating, we must look to the Lord alone to liberate us: the power is His. When David cried to Him, He lifted him up out of the horrible pit and the miry clay, and set his feet on a rock, and put a new song of praise and thanksgiving into his heart. So that Jesus, in His power, is "the same yesterday, and to-day, and for ever."

If you are hemmed up in providence, and cannot see your way, look to the Lord and His power to liberate you. All the gold and silver is His, and, when He wants it, He can have it out of a fish's mouth; all hearts are in his hand, and He can turn them as rivers of water. Look to the Lord; all power is with Him. "Cast thy burden upon the LORD, he will sustain thee" "Casting all your care upon him, for he careth for you." My aim in labouring in the ministry of the word is to set forth

our Lord Jesus Christ, to exalt Him. and enable you to increase
your confidence in Him, in His power, in His ability, and in His
glorious all-sufficiency.

III.   We now observe, "Jesus Christ" is "the same yesterday,
and to-day, and for ever," *in His salvation.* A large field opens
to us here, but we can only briefly glance at it. The salvation
that we have in Jesus Christ is not a changing or uncertain
salvation; it is like Himself, "the same yesterday, and to-day,
and for ever." Hearken to the voice of God; there is such a
solemnity and majesty in His word when the Holy Spirit is
pleased to apply it with power to the mind: "Israel shall be
saved in the LORD with an everlasting salvation." Jesus has
"obtained eternal redemption for us." Abraham rejoiced in
Jesus and His salvation; he rejoiced to see His day, and he saw
it, and was glad. Jacob died in the enjoyment of this salvation:
"The angel of the covenant that hath redeemed me from all
evil, bless the lads." Job exulted in it: "I know that my
Redeemer liveth." The church, in the days of the prophet
Isaiah, sang of it: "Behold, God is my salvation, I will trust, and
not be afraid." Come into the New Testament; it is still Jesus:
"Neither is there salvation in any other; for there is none other
name under heaven given among men whereby we must be
saved," but the name of Jesus.

O the everlasting salvation that we have in Jesus Christ! He
is the same, and will be the same for ever and ever! and, the
righteousness He has wrought out for us is like Himself; it is an
everlasting righteousness. It covered our first parents. It is
true, they sewed fig leaves together to cover themselves, but
God rejected them, as He will reject our self-righteousness, and
clothed them with the skins of beasts that had probably been
slain in sacrifice. Abraham had to look to this Jesus for
righteousness, and so had the prophets, and so have we. It is an
everlasting righteousness, covering all the election of grace in
ages gone by, covering them all today, and that will cover them
all tomorrow; making them accepted in the presence of a holy
God. As it is written, we are "accepted in the Beloved," beheld
all fair and perfect in the Lord Jesus. And as respects the blood
of this salvation, it is "the blood of the everlasting covenant."
All the church of God in ages past have been purged from sin
in the blood of Jesus; and the church of God at this day is
looking by faith to the blood of the slaughtered Lamb; and it
will be the same to us tomorrow and as long as we live; and

when we have gone to glory we shall shout, "Victory through the blood of the Lamb and the word of His testimony! That blood will still maintain its power.

> Dear dying Lamb! thy precious blood
> Shall never lose its power.

It has had a power, it has a power now, and it will have a power,

> Till all the ransomed church of God
> Be saved, to sin no more!   Cowper

"Jesus Christ the same yesterday, and to-day, and for ever." As the Church's advocate in heaven to plead her cause Christ has taken possession of the inheritance in our nature. He

> Looks like a Lamb that has been slain,
> And wears his priesthood still;

and He enables His people to look to Him, and to commit their cause into His hands. The child of God may sometimes think that he is going backwards, or else standing still; but there is such a thing as taking deep root, growing upwards and downwards at the same time. You may be sure that religion is progressing in our souls if we are getting every day more and more out of love with ourselves, and feeling more and more our need of the Lord Jesus Christ. If we are cleaving to Him, hoping in Him, panting after Him, longing for Him, and desiring to be "found in him," conformed to His image, to live to His honour and glory. It is Jesus by His Holy Spirit that causes the Dagon of self to fall, and exalts Himself in our hearts and affections; "Jesus Christ the same yesterday, and today, and for ever."

It may be that I may never speak to you in the name of Jesus any more; but if I do not, Jesus Christ still remains. If His ministering servants die and His people die, Jesus lives; and He ever had His witnesses, and ever will have. He ever had a seed to serve Him, and a generation to call Him blessed; and in spite of sin, men and devils, He will have; and He will carry on His work till all the ransomed of the Lord, the whole election of grace, are gathered in. "Then shall the end be," the world be burned up, the judgment take place, and the spouse be for ever in the presence of the dear Redeemer. Amen.

10

Faithfulness and Longsuffering

PREACHED AT ZION CHAPEL, TROWBRIDGE
OCTOBER AND NOVEMBER, 1834

The Lord is not slack concerning His promise, as some men count slackness; but is long-suffering to us-ward, not willing that any should perish, but that all should come to repentance." (2 Peter 3. 9.)

In the religious world there is a great diversity of opinion concerning Christ. Some are crying out, "Lo, here is Christ" and others, "Lo, he is there;" but we are exhorted by our Lord to "believe them not," but to "try the spirits, whether they be of God; because many false prophets are gone out into the world." The great error of many is they take their own sentiments of the word of God, and labour to make the Bible speak their fleshly whims and notions, instead of taking their principles from the word of God and strive to ascertain the beauty and harmony that shine forth in the Scriptures. For instance; the Arian and the Socinian, who deny the personal Godhead of Christ, refer principally to those texts that speak of His manhood, and then deny the great and glorious mystery of godliness, "God manifest in the flesh." Then again, the Arminians, who fight against the doctrine of election and particular redemption and vindicate the universal scheme, refer to our text and passages of a similar import, and labour to make them speak their sentiments, without carefully examining the connexion in which such texts stand. Were they to do this, under the Holy Spirit's teaching, they would find their meaning is very different; as I shall endeavour to prove.

From the words of our text, I will, with the help of the Lord, take notice of the following things:—

   I.   The Lord is not slack concerning the fulfilment of His promises as some men count slackness;

   II.   The Lord is long-suffering to us-ward;

   III.   He is not willing that any should perish;

   IV.   He wills that all should come to repentance.

I.

The Lord is not slack concerning the fulfilment of His promises as some men count slackness.

(1.)   The promise particularly alluded to is that of *Christ's second coming to judgment;* and it is one of those "exceeding great and precious promises" that our Lord has given us. He told His disciples that He would go and prepare a place for them; and He made a promise to comfort them in their trouble saying, "I will come again, and receive you unto myself; that where I am, there ye may be also." This is what the saints of the Lord long for, as Paul did when he said, "Having a desire to depart, and be with Christ, which is far better," than being here in this "body of sin and death," and this world of sorrow and woe.

When our Lord ascended up on high, having "led captivity captive," His disciples looked steadfastly upon Him as He went up, till a cloud received Him out of their sight. And while they looked stedfastly toward heaven as He went up, behold, two men (or angels in the form of men) stood by them in white apparel; (making a promise of our Lord's second coming) said, Ye men of Galilee, why stand ye gazing up into heaven? this same Jesus which is taken up from you into heaven, shall so come in like manner as ye have seen him go into heaven." Whatever scoffers may say against Christ's second coming and the judgment of the great day, this word of promise, spoken by angels, shall stand, "and every transgression and disobedience shall receive a just recompence of reward," in that great and awful day "when the Lord Jesus shall be revealed from heaven with his mighty angels, in flaming fire, taking vengeance on them that know not God, and that obey not the gospel of our Lord Jesus Christ; who shall be punished with everlasting destruction from the presence of the Lord, and from the glory of his power." (2 Th. 1. 7-9.)

This is the awful and doleful side of the question. But the apostle directs our attention in the next verse to another and more glorious end that our Lord has in view in His second coming. "He shall come to be glorified in his saints, and to be admired in all them that believe." Have we not often admired His beauty and glory when, by the eye of faith, we have seen Him who is invisible; for the goings forth of our God and King are to be seen in His sanctuary, or His church in her militant state. Thus saith the Lord, "Thine eyes shall see the king in his beauty; they shall behold the land that is very far off." Though it is but "through a glass darkly," yet one glimpse of His beauty constrains us to say, "Whom have I in heaven but thee? and there is none upon earth that I desire besides thee." For He is the chief amongst ten thousand, and the altogether lovely. If this be the joy we feel when we see but a glimpse of His beauty, and that through a glass darkly, what will be the joy of our hearts when we behold His face in righteousness, without a glass or cloud between? We shall then admire His beauty, and adore His majesty for ever and ever with joy indescribable.

In the verses preceding our text, the apostle Peter brings forward the arguments that the scoffers of his day used against Christ's second coming, saying, as they did in a contemptuous manner, "Where is the promise of his coming? for since the fathers fell asleep, all things continue as they were from the beginning of the creation." "For this," says Peter, "they willingly are ignorant of, that, by the word of God the heavens were of old, and the earth standing out of the water and in the water; whereby the world that then was, being overflowed with water, perished: but the heavens and the earth, which are now, by the same word are kept in store, reserved unto fire against the day of judgment and perdition of ungodly men." Whatever infidels may say, "the day of the Lord will come as a thief in the night." "For the Lord himself shall descend from heaven with a shout, with the voice of the archangel, and with the trump of God." He shall "sit upon the throne of his glory, and before him shall be gathered all nations." Yea, these

> Sinners must now come forth,
> And stand before the Lord,
> Whose word they scorned on earth,
> Whose children they abhorred.

(Burnham)

And these shall go away "into everlasting fire, prepared for the devil and his angels," where their worm shall not die, neither shall their fire be quenched.

How amazingly different is the state of the true Christian, who is looking for, and hasting unto, the coming of the day of God. Having felt the sentence of the killing letter of God's law in his conscience, a knowledge of sin has revived. He has died to all hope of going to heaven on the ground of his own works, and like the Psalmist, has cried unto the Lord out of the horrible pit; and the Lord, in answer to his prayer, has lifted him out of the miry clay and set his feet for eternity upon the Rock of Ages, being washed in the blood of the Lamb. Clothed in the wedding garment, and sealed with the Holy Spirit of promise, which is the earnest of our inheritance and pledge of future glory, the believer is ready to exclaim, "Come, Lord Jesus, come quickly!"

We live in a day in which much is said about Christ's second coming and the millennium, or Christ's thousand years' reign with His saints on earth. Some men are so full of this doctrine that it is the principal topic they dwell on, and they labour in it as if they meant to frighten their hearers out of their senses. But the most needful thing for us to inquire after is this — are we born again and made new creatures in Christ Jesus? Have we the Spirit of Christ? Are we complete in Christ? Have we the oil of divine grace in our hearts, and are our lamps burning? If so, let the Lord come soon or late, we are ready to enter into the marriage supper of the Lamb; and it will be of little advantage to us whether we reign with Him on earth or in heaven; for if we are where Jesus is, we shall be happy. For in His presence there is fulness of joy; and at His right hand there are pleasures for evermore.

(2). The Lord is not slack in the fulfilment of *His promise as the God of nature;* for He has said, "While the earth remaineth, seedtime and harvest, and cold and heat, and summer and winter, day and night, shall not cease." (Gen. 8. 22.) We are all witnesses of the faithfulness of God to this promise, for we see the seasons regularly roll round. After a cold and dreary winter, during which the trees and plants have appeared withered and dead, have we not beheld the return of spring — the "time of the singing of birds" — when the sun has gone forth in his strength and warmed the earth, and the Lord has commanded the early and latter rain to water and replenish it? We have seen the trees budding and blossoming and bringing forth fruit, and the earth yielding her increase, filling our barns with food for man and beast.

May the Lord make us thankful for His goodness as the God of nature, and enable us so to use the good things of this life as not to abuse them, giving thanks to His name.

(3). Our God has not been slack in the fulfilment of *His promise made to Noah that he would never more destroy the whole earth with a flood of water.*

As a token of His faithfulness, God has "set his bow (commonly called the rainbow) in the clouds" of heaven. When we see it in all its beautiful colours, it is a silent but true preacher of the faithfulness of God to His promise.

The Lord, speaking by the prophet Isaiah, for the comfort of His people, says, "In a little wrath I hid my face from thee for a moment; but with everlasting kindness will I have mercy on thee. For this is as the waters of Noah unto me; for as I have sworn that the waters of Noah should no more go over the earth; so have I sworn that I would not be wroth with thee, nor rebuke thee. For the mountains shall depart, and the hills be removed, but my kindness shall not depart from thee, neither shall the covenant of my peace be removed, saith the LORD that hath mercy on thee." (Is. 54. 8-10.)

When we have looked at this bow in the clouds, has it not, even when our minds have been in darkness, been the means in the hand of the Holy Spirit of leading our hearts to Him, who has said, "Who is among you that feareth the LORD, that obeyeth the voice of his servant, that walketh in darkness and hath no light? let him trust in the name of the LORD, and stay upon his God." For there is nowhere else for us to look for comfort but to Him who is everlastingly the same in all His attributes and perfections, whatever be the state or frame of our minds. "For if we believe not, yet he abideth faithful; he cannot deny himself." Therefore we can at times sing, even when in darkness —

> The gospel bears my spirit up:
> A faithful and unchanging God
> Lays the foundation of my hope,
> In oaths, and promises, and blood.

(Watts)

The Babel builders, disbelieving the promise God made to Noah, began to build their tower which was to reach from earth to heaven, and by means of which they might escape another deluge should one come. But the Lord was displeased with what they did; and a Triune Jehovah came down from heaven, and confounded their language and defeated their design. This He always does with the fears of His people, overthrowing all their projects proceeding from unbelief and carnal reason. Unbelief and carnal reason, like Babel, must fall, but the faithfulness of the Lord shall stand for ever, for it is established in the very heavens.

(4). God the Father is not slack concerning *the promises He's made to the Lord Jesus Christ, the church's Head and Mediator.*

In reading the Scriptures we find many promises made by the Father to the Son, assuring Him that He should have and enjoy all the purchase of His blood. In the second Psalm, the Father, speaking to Christ, said, "Yet have I set my king upon my holy hill of Zion. I will declare the decree; the LORD hath said unto me, Thou art my Son; this day have I begotten thee. Ask of me, and I shall give thee the heathen for thine inheritance, and the uttermost parts of the earth for thy possession." By the heathen and the uttermost parts of the earth are meant God's elect, scattered abroad amongst the Gentile nations. They are Christ's "other sheep. . . . which are not of this fold: them also I must bring, and they shall hear my voice; and there shall be one fold, and one shepherd." (John 10. 16.) Wherever the King's banished ones are cast in the cloudy and dark day of their unregeneracy, the Lord knows where they are: "Having this seal, the Lord knoweth them that are his."

Hearken to the voice of the great Shepherd, speaking by the prophet Ezekiel, "For thus saith the Lord GOD, Behold, I, even I, will both search my sheep, and seek them out. As a shepherd seeketh out his flock in the day that he is among his sheep that are scattered; so will I seek out my sheep, and will deliver them out of all places where they have been scattered in the cloudy and dark day." (Ezek. 34. 11-12). In the next verse what a display of the discriminating nature of God's grace in the effectual calling of His people, and how evident it is that He is found of them that sought Him not, and made manifest unto them that looked not for Him. "And I will bring them out from the people, and will gather them from the countries, and will bring them to their own land." (v. 13). The Lord does not say, I will give them an opportunity of coming unto me, if they will but exercise the freedom of their own will. No, but He "will seek that which was lost, and bring again that which was driven away." (ver. 16).

Some may say, But how if they will not come to Christ, and be gathered by Him? To answer this we are led to another promise that the Father has made to Christ. "Thy people shall be willing in the day of thy power." (Ps. 110. 3). Observe the beauty and force of this passage. The Father, speaking to Christ, says, "Thy people"—those that I gave Thee in covenant love, whom Thou hast engaged to redeem by Thy blood — "*shall be willing* in the day of thy power." See how gloriously this promise was fulfilled at the day of Pentecost, when the apostles were in so eminent a manner endued with power from on high, and when the word spoken by them entered into the hearts of the murderers of Christ; for, being pricked in their heart, they said to Peter and the other apostles, "Men and brethren, what shall we do?" Peter preached to them the doctrine of repentance and of baptism in the name of Jesus Christ, that they might receive the remission of sins; and they that gladly received the word willingly bowed to the sceptre of that Jesus whom they had crucified and slain, manifesting their love to Him by being baptized in His name. And the same day there were added unto the number of the disciples of Jesus of Nazareth about three thousand souls. (Acts 2. 31-41.) What a proof of the power of the Lord attending the preaching of His word by these illiterate fishermen, and of the faithfulness of the Father to His promise, saying, "Thy people shall be willing in the day of thy power."

Solomon says, "Where the word of a king is, there is power." Our Jesus is King of kings, and Lord of lords; so that where His voice is there is the greatest of all power; and His voice is often heard, and His power felt, in the ministry of His word by His ministers to this day. For the Lord is riding forth upon the white horse of His everlasting gospel, conquering and to conquer. At His word the stoutest heart must tremble as Saul of Tarsus did (Acts 9. 6). "And the loftiness of man shall be bowed down, and the haughtiness of men shall be made low: and the LORD alone shall be exalted in that day," — to wit, the day of the Lord's power. His grace shall reign in the effectual calling of His people until the headstone is brought to the building of mercy, when the cry shall be with shouting, "Grace, grace, unto it."

This leads us to another of the promises the Father has made to the Lord Jesus Christ, which we have on record in the prophecy of Isaiah. "He shall see his seed, he shall prolong his days, and the pleasure of the LORD shall prosper in his hand." There is a seed here spoken of, which is Christ's spiritual seed. This seed Paul speaks of: "Except the Lord of Sabaoth had left us a seed, we had been as Sodoma, and been like unto Gomorrah." (Rom. 9. 29). This is a quotation of Paul's from Isaiah 1. 9; and what Paul calls a seed, the prophet calls a very small remnant. Later, Paul calls it "a remnant according to the election of grace." (Rom. 11. 5.)

Christ is the Father's first elect, and all His spiritual seed were chosen in Him who is the corn of wheat that fell into the ground and died, but did not abide alone, but sprung up again and is bringing forth His spiritual seed unto this day. "And he shall prolong his days", till they are all "born again, not of corruptible seed, but of incorruptible, by the word of God, which liveth and abideth for ever." Being born of God, they are "a seed to serve him, and a generation to call him blessed." This spiritual seed of Christ, the Father tells us He will "make to endure for ever, and his throne as the days of heaven (Ps. 39. 29). When the harvest is gathered in, and they are all brought into the garner above, both men and angels shall shout the harvest home, and the Triune Jehovah rejoice to hear.

Another promise that the Father has made to Christ is, "He shall see of the travail of his soul, and shall be satisfied." (Isa. 53. 11.) By the travail of the Redeemer's soul, we are to understand the sufferings He endured in working out our salvation. The prophet Isaiah beheld Him "travelling in the greatness of his strength," and treading in the winepress of His Father's wrath, and of the people there was none with Him. In this prophecy, we behold Jesus in the garden of Gethsemane, resisting unto blood, striving against sin, and we hear Him say, "My soul is exceeding sorrowful, even unto death." If we look at Him on the cross, we behold the sword of divine justice unsheathed against Him, and His soul made an offering for the sins of His people. Having thus travailed in soul, "he shall see his seed. . . . and shall be satisfied." As a woman, after the sharp pains of labour are over, having brought forth a son, looks on him with joy and satisfaction, and rejoices " that a man is born into the world" (John 16. 21), so the Redeemer, after the travail of His soul, shall rejoice to see the purchase of His blood, plucked as a brand out of the fire, humbled at His feet with a broken and contrite heart, determined to venture their souls' eternal all into Jesus' hands, and to take up their cross and to follow Him through evil and through good report, until they sit down with Him in His kingdom of glory above. For neither will the Lord nor His people ever be fully satisfied till they are all enthroned together in the realms of bliss to part no more.

Some people tell us there are of the purchase of Christ's blood now in hell. If so, there is a slackness in the Father's promise, and it falls to the ground unaccomplished; for Christ will never be satisfied if He be deprived of His purchase, as is evident from His intercessory prayer, "Father, I will that they also, whom thou hast given me, be with me where I am; that they may behold my glory." So, as Christ's will is that they all shall be with Him where He is, He cannot be satisfied, nor will the Father be faithful, if any be lost. I speak it with reverence; before this can take place, heaven must sink, and hell must rise and triumph over the throne of God and the Lamb; and this can never, never be.

In order to more clearly show the force of the argument which arises out of these statements, I will use a simile. The greatest part of you, my friends, in this large congregation are labouring men, who earn your bread by the sweat of your brow. You go to your work on Monday morning, and having done your duty to your master, not with eye-service, as pleasing men, but God, when Saturday night comes you go to your master's pay table and receive your wages, and return home with it. After this you go to market and buy those things that you and your family need. Then you return home, and, as prudence dictates, examine whether you have all the goods you have purchased, when you discover that this and the other thing is wanting. And are you satisfied? No; the husband says to the wife, "My dear, did not we buy this and that? but, behold, they are not here; we have been robbed of them, or have lost them." So there is nothing but dissatisfaction. But if, on the other hand, on examination, you find all the purchase there, you are satisfied. If this be the case in these minor things, can we for a moment suppose that the great Redeemer will be satisfied to lose *His* purchase? O! no. But more of this in another part of our discourse.

(5). The Father is not slack concerning *the promises He has made to His church and people in Christ.*

All the promises that our covenant God and Father has made to His people are made to them in Christ. "For all the promises of God in him are yea, and in him Amen, unto the glory of God by us." (2. Cor. 1. 20.) Had the promises been made to us on the ground of something being done by us, on condition of which our God would bless us, we should be in despair of enjoying the promised blessing. For we who know the plague of our own hearts cannot kneel down before God, and plead with Him to bless us upon the ground of any worth or worthiness there is in us. It is the self-righteous pharisee who pleads with God to bless him upon the ground of his own doings, saying, "God, I thank thee, that I am not as other men are, extortioners, unjust, adulterers, or even as this publican. I fast twice in the week, I give tithes of all I possess." (Lk. 18. 11, 12.) Can any of you, my hearers, kneel down before the Lord your Maker, and like this pharisee, tell the Lord a good tale of yourselves and your own doings? If you can, your hearts are like Simon Magus's not right in the sight of God; for you are in the gall of bitterness and bonds of iniquity. Whatever fair show you may make in the flesh, you are but whited walls and painted sepulchres, appearing outwardly beautiful, "but within are full of dead men's bones, and of all uncleanness."

How different is the conduct of the true Christian, who knows and daily feels his own weakness and infirmities! Hear his language when pleading with the Lord for His blessing. "Behold now, I have taken upon me to speak unto the Lord, which am but dust and ashes." "I am not worthy of the least of all the mercies, and of all the truth, which thou hast showed unto thy servant." "We do not present our supplications before thee for our own righteousness, but for thy great mercies." If ever we rise in ourselves the breadth of a straw above the prayer of the poor publican, "God be merciful to me a sinner," we are too high, and must come down. The Christian begins with this prayer, he has to use it all his pilgrimage through, and it will be his prayer on a dying bed.

There is nothing in us, or done by us, that we can plead before the Lord for His blessing. As we, in the matter of our justification before God, renounce everything but the person, blood, and righteousness of Christ, so, in our approaches to the Majesty of heaven, we must renounce everything but the name, the blood, and righteousness of Jesus, who for our comfort said, "Verily, verily, I say unto you, Whatsoever ye shall ask the Father in my name, he will give it you." When we come before God, and look to ourselves, we tremble, and wonder the Lord does not cut us down, as cumberers of the ground. But when by a living faith we are enabled to look to Christ, we feel something of that humble boldness Paul speaks of: "Having therefore, brethren, boldness to enter into the holiest by the blood of Jesus, by a new and living way, which he consecrated for us, through the veil, that is to say, his flesh." (Heb. 10. 19,20.) This new and living way which is Christ and Him crucified is the only ground upon which we can plead the promises of God, and look to Him for His blessing; and Christ and Him crucified is the only ground upon which a just and holy God can meet and bless such guilty sinners as we are; for in Christ, "mercy and truth are met together, righteousness and peace have kissed each other."

When God made promise to Jacob, it was from the top of the ladder which united heaven and earth; and this ladder is none other than our Immanuel, in His human and divine natures, the one Mediator between God and man. When the Lord spoke to Jacob, Jacob was at the foot of the ladder, and his God spoke to him from the top, and made him a promise, saying, "Behold, I am with thee, and will keep thee in all places whither thou goest, ... for I will not leave thee until I have done that which I have spoken to thee of." (Gen. 28. 15.) Oh, may we often be like Jacob at the foot of this blessed ladder, Jesus Christ; and may we, as Jacob did, hear our heavenly Father speaking to us by promise from the top of this ladder, that our souls may be refreshed, and our spiritual strength renewed, as his was. This Bethel visit Jacob never forgot to his dying day; and the promise made to him stands and shines in the Scriptures as a sunbeam for the comfort of God's spiritual Israel in every age.

Moses, having proved the Lord to be faithful to His word, brings this promise forward to encourage his successor, Joshua; saying unto him, in the sight of all Israel, "Be strong, and of good courage,... for the Lord will be with thee, he will not fail thee, neither forsake thee: fear not, neither be dismayed."

(Deut. 31. 7, 8.) After the death of Moses, the Lord makes the same promise to Joshua, saying, "As I was with Moses, so I will be with thee: I will not fail thee, nor forsake thee."

The prophet Samuel, having proved the faithfulness of God to His promises, speaking for the encouragement of Israel, said, "The LORD will not forsake his people for his great name's sake: because it hath pleased the LORD to make them his people." David brings the same promise forward to encourage his son Solomon in the building of the temple: "Be strong and of good courage, and do it: fear not, nor be dismayed: for the LORD God, even my God, will be with thee; he will not fail thee, nor forsake thee." David further says, "I have been young and now am old; yet have I not seen the righteous forsaken, nor his seed begging bread." (Ps. 37. 25.)

Isaiah brings the same undertaking: "Fear thou not; for I am with thee; be not dismayed, for I am thy God: I will strengthen thee; yea, I will help thee; yea, I will uphold thee with the right hand of my righteousness." (Is. 41. 10.) And in verse 14 it is said, "Fear not, thou worm Jacob, and ye men of Israel." So you see, when God made promise to Jacob from the top of the ladder, it was made not only to him but to all his spiritual seed. The prophet Hosea confirms this idea, by telling us that the Lord found Jacob "in Bethel, and there he spake with us." (Hos. 12. 4.) Mark the words of the prophet; not only did the Lord speak with Jacob, but He spake with *us*. Paul, in his Epistle to the Hebrews, having the sweet enjoyment of this promise in his own soul, brings it forward in the following soul-animating language: "Let your conversation be without covetousness; and be content with such things as ye have; for he hath said, I will never leave thee nor forsake thee." In Dr. Doddridge's paraphrase of this text, the term never is repeated three times. Truly, a triune Jehovah will never leave nor forsake His people; "So that we may boldly say, The Lord is my helper, and I will not fear what man shall do unto me." (Heb. 13. 5, 6.)

Joshua, in his exhortation to the people before his death, comes forward as a witness for God, and appeals to the consciences of the people in reference to the faithfulness of God to His promises: "Behold, this day I am going the way of all the earth; and ye know in all your hearts and in all your souls, that not one thing hath failed of all the good things which the LORD your God spake concerning you; all are come to pass unto you, and not one thing hath failed thereof" (Josh. 23. 14.)

So you see, there is no slackness in our God, concerning the fulfilment of His promise as some men count slackness.

(6). There is however another principle that we must notice in this part of our discourse. In order that we may prove each for ourselves that the Lord is not slack concerning his promises, *we must be brought in our experience, into those circumstances which will make us feel the need of the things which our God has promised, and be enabled, under the Holy Spirit's influence, to plead the promises by faith, and rest upon them*; as the following instances left on record, abundantly prove.

Abraham is called by the Lord to go forth from his own country and his kindred and his father's house, and to turn his back on their idolatrous worship. This must have been a great trial to him but, for the support of his mind, the Lord made him a promise of the land of Canaan, that his seed should be as the stars of heaven, and that in his seed all the families of the earth should be blessed. He had not only the promise, but the Lord gave him faith in the promise; so it was by faith in the promise and in the faithfulness of God that he went forth not knowing whither he went; and as he travelled along the promise was the comfort and the support of his mind. (Gen. 12; Heb. 11. 8.)

For a further trial of the patriarch's faith, the Lord allowed Sarah to go childless, until Abraham and she began to think there was a slackness in the Lord's fulfilling His promise; and from a principle of unbelief, Sarah persuaded Abraham to go in unto her handmaid, Hagar. Abraham complied, and Hagar was with child by her master. But instead of these carnal efforts bringing about the promise of God, they brought only confusion into the family, as our unbelief and carnal efforts that we may use to forward God's purposes and promises do to this day. The Lord does not need such carnal means to enable Him to fulfil His promises.

The promise is still delayed, and at length it ceased to be with Sarah after the manner of women, and Abraham was as good as dead; and now, when all fleshly hopes are cut off, a faithful God renews His promise: "Sarah shall have a son, in whom all the families of the earth shall be blessed." Abraham's faith is revived, and instead of counting a slackness in the Lord, Paul tells us that he "against hope believed in hope; . . . . and being not weak in faith, he considered not his own body now dead, when he was about an hundred years old, neither yet the deadness of Sarah's womb. He staggered not at the promise of God through unbelief; but was strong in faith, giving glory to God. And being fully persuaded that, what he had promised, he was able also to perform." (Rom. 4. 18-21.) Sarah, at the set time, brings forth a son, even Isaac, who was a type of our Lord Jesus Christ in many things.

Paul, in setting forth the faithfulness of God to His promises, refers to His promise to Abraham. "For when God made promise to Abraham, because he could swear by no greater, he sware by himself, saying, Surely, blessing I will bless thee, and multiplying I will multiply thee. And so after he had patiently endured, he obtained the promise. For men verily swear by the greater: and an oath for confirmation is to them an end of all strife." (Heb. 6. 13-16.) That the promise made to Abraham, the father of the faithful, still stands for the comfort of all his spiritual seed, whether Jews or Gentiles, is evident from the manner in which the apostle pursues the subject: "Where God, willing more abundantly to shew unto the heirs of promise the immutability of his counsel, confirmed it by an oath that by two immutable things, in which it was impossible for God to lie, we might have a strong consolation, who have fled for refuge to lay hold upon the hope set before us: which hope we have as an anchor of the soul, both sure and stedfast, and which entereth into that within the veil, whither the forerunner is for us entered, even Jesus, made an high priest for ever, after the order of Melchisedec." (Heb. 6. 17-20.)

As a further proof that we must be brought into those circumstances that will make us feel our need of the promised blessing, I refer you to Jacob, of whom I have already spoken. He stood in need of the promise that his God made to him at Bethel, and it was his comfort and support as he went on his journey. But we find him in greater need of the Lord's help when he was returning from his father-in-law's with all that appertained to him, when the messenger told him that his brother Esau was coming against him with an army of four hundred men. This is the time of Jacob's greatest trouble, for it is said he was greatly afraid, fearing that Esau would smite him with the mother and the children. In this day of trouble, he uses that blessed weapon, all-prayer. He sends all that he has over Jordan, and he is left behind to spread his case before the Lord. Thus it is, when we are in any particular trouble, we must have the matter over with the Lord in secret, as Jacob had.

As Jacob was pleading with the Lord to appear for him, and make a way for his escape, the Holy Spirit (the remembrancer) brought afresh to his mind the promise his God had made to him at Bethel, and by faith he pleaded it, saying, "Thou saidst, I will surely do thee good." And as he was pleading the promise, there wrestled a man with him, which was none other than Christ, the Angel of the covenant; and He said, "Let me go, for the day breaketh." But wrestling Jacob, having fast hold of the promise by faith, said, "I will not let thee go, except thou bless me;" thou who hast all hearts in thine own hands, and canst turn them as the rivers of water, thou must appear for me, and deliver me from the hands of my brother Esau. As Jacob was thus pleading with the Lord, the Angel said to him, "What is thy name? And he said, Jacob." But the Angel of the covenant said, "Thy name shall be called no more Jacob, but Israel; for as a prince hast thou power with God and with men, and hast prevailed." (Gen. 32.) Jacob prayed the Lord to be a present help in the time of his trouble; and his God, as the breaker of Israel, went before him, and broke down the enmity of Esau's heart; so that when Jacob lifted up his eyes and saw him, Esau ran to meet him and instead of frowns there was a look of affection, and instead of blows, kissing and weeping. Truly it may be said, "What hath God wrought."

We see from this account, the blessedness of leaving all our concerns in the Lord's hands. "Cast thy burden upon the LORD, and he shall sustain thee."

We also find Paul himself brought into circumstances where he stood in special need of the promise of God to support his mind. He had an abundant revelation, being caught up into the third heaven, and hearing unspeakable things, which it is not lawful for a man to utter; and he tells us that lest he should be exalted above measure, through the abundance of the revelations, there was given to him a thorn in the flesh, the messenger of Satan, to buffet him. This thorn in the flesh, Paul did not like — it was painful and grievous to flesh and blood; and he besought the Lord thrice that it might depart from him. But this was not his Master's will. So Paul had not, not because he asked not, but because he asked amiss. When we pray to escape the path of tribulation, we pray contrary to the word and will of our heavenly Father, who has said, "In the world ye shall have tribulation." It is "through much tribulation that we must enter the kingdom of heaven;" and they that are there, enthroned in glory, are such as "have come up out of great tribulation." William Huntington was wont to observe, "They that are out of the path of tribulation are out of the way." Although the Lord would not remove Paul's thorn in the flesh, He gave him a promise to support his mind, saying unto him, "My grace is sufficient for thee, for my strength is made perfect in weakness." This enabled him to glory in the path of tribulation, and to say, When I am weakest in myself, then I am the strongest in the Lord, and in the power of His might. (2 Cor. 12.)

There is no state into which we can be brought that the grace and promise of God is not sufficient to support our mind while we are exercised therewith. Paul could do all things through Christ which strengthened him. On this subject, the poet sweetly sings —

> Let me but hear my Saviour say,
>   Strength shall be equal to thy day;
> Then I rejoice in deep distress,
>   Leaning on all-sufficient grace.

(Watts)

If we refer to a few of the promises, we shall find that they are made for the comfort of the saints in their troubles. "But now thus saith the LORD that created thee, O Jacob, and he that formed thee, O Israel; Fear not, for I have redeemed thee, I have called thee by thy name, thou art mine. When thou passest through the waters, I will be with thee." (Is. 43. 1,2.) To prove this promise true we must be brought into the waters of affliction and adversity, and pass through them as Israel did through the Red Sea, and we must have the Lord with us as Israel had in the sea, to keep us from being overflowed and to hold us up. "When thou walkest through the fire thou shalt not be burned; neither shall the flames kindle upon thee." (v.3.) There is to be fire-work; for the Lord has chosen Zion "in the furnace of affliction" and he "will bring the third part through the fire." So we need not to think it strange concerning the fiery trial which is to try us as though some strange thing happened unto us. There is the fire of persecution, and into this fire Shadrach, Meshech, and Abednego were cast, because they would not fall down and worship Nebuchadnezzar's golden god. And when they were cast into the fire, the Son of God went in with them. and commanded the flames, so that not a hair of their head was singed, nor their coats changed, nor the smell of fire passed on them. Thus they proved that the Lord was not slack concerning His promise.

There is the fire of temptation, and in this we must be tried, "if need be, ye are in heaviness through manifold temptation;" and this is for the trial of our faith, which is "more precious than gold that perisheth, though it be tried with fire." In this fire our Lord was keenly tried when tempted of the devil in the wilderness, that He might be an able succourer of His tempted family. For their comfort He has said that no temptation shall happen to them but such as is common to men, and that He will with the temptation make a way for their escape that they may be able to bear it.

There is the fire of afflictive dispensations in providence, in which Job was so sorely tried.

Our Lord has been afflicted in all our affliction, and we have Him with us to comfort and support us in our afflictions. Many of the Lord's family can testify that they have most of the Lord's presence with them in their greatest trials, and thus have proved the Lord to be faithful.

Our Lord has His fire in Zion, and His furnace in Jerusalem (Is. 31. 9); for He tells us that "it is impossible but that offences must come, but woe unto him through whom they come." This is the most painful fire when the most excellent of the earth are as pricking thorns in each others' eyes and sides. Paul calls it biting and devouring one another: and he exhorts such to take heed that they be not consumed one of another. But whatever fire we may be in, our Lord sits "as a refiner and purifier of silver: and he shall purify the sons of Levi, and purge them as gold and silver, that they may offer unto the LORD an offering in righteousness." (Mal. 3. 3.) So we shall ever find the Lord to be faithful to His promise, whatever fire or water we may have to pass through.

In another promise, our God says he will bring the blind by a way they know not, and will lead them in paths that they have not known, and will make darkness light before them, and crooked things straight. These things will He do unto them, and not forsake them. (Is. 42. 16.) Such as have no darkness to complain of, nor crooked things to be exercised with, can never prove the faithfulness of the Lord to this promise. But this is not the lot of the Lord's family, for they have often to walk in darkness and cannot see their way, and they have many crooked things, both within and without, and have to say with Israel of old, "Neither know we what to do: but our eyes are upon thee." (2 Chron. 20. 12.) When they are in this state, it is sweet to be enabled to obey the exhortation of the Lord, "Be still and know that I am God" "For this (faithful) God is our God for ever and ever; he will be our guide even unto death."

II

We now pass on to the second part of the subject, which is to show that **the Lord is long-suffering to us-ward.**

(1). *We will inquire who the "us-ward" are to* whom the Lord is said to be long-suffering.

They are undoubtedly the persons to whom Peter writes his epistles, including himself.Let us turn, then, to the first epistle, and see to whom he wrote: "Peter, an apostle of Jesus Christ, to the strangers scattered throughout Pontus, Galatia, Cappadocia, Asia, and Bithynia;" and he then gives them the honoured appellation of "Elect, according to the foreknowledge of God the Father." In the second chapter of this epistle, he calls them "a chosen generation, a royal priesthood, an holy nation, a peculiar people, that they should show forth the praises of him who hath called them out of darkness into his marvellous light."

It is worthy of remark, that the pronouns us and we, so often used by the apostles, in their epistles, are no other than the Lord's chosen people, to whom the precious truths contained in those epistles belong. As a confirmation of this fact, let me refer you to the following texts, in which these two terms, us and we, are often used : "Blessed be the God and Father of our Lord Jesus Christ, who hath blessed us with all spiritual blessings in heavenly places in Christ, according as he hath chosen us in him before the foundation of the world, that we should be holy and without blame before him in love, having predestinated us unto the adoption of children by Jesus Christ to himself, according to the good pleasure of his will." (Eph. 1 3-5.) "But let us who are of the day be sober, for God hath not appointed us to wrath, but to obtain salvation by our Lord Jesus Christ." (1 Thess. 5. 8. 9.) "Who hath saved us and called us with an holy calling, not according to our works, but according to his own purpose and grace, which was given us in Christ Jesus before the world began."(2 Tim. 1. 9.) You see, my friends, from these passages, and many more that might be produced, that the "us-ward" in our text are the objects of God's everlasting, electing love; and that their election is not founded upon any foreseen worth or worthiness in the creature, as the procuring cause of it, will be seen from the characters unto whom the Lord has been long-suffering.

(2). *We will now speak of the long-suffering of God to His people.*

(i). The Lord is long-suffering to His people *before they are called by His grace.* This is evident from the following characters which we have left on record.

Behold the long-suffering of God to Manasseh, King of Judah. The idolatrous worship which his father Hezekiah had demolished, Manasseh re-established; and, as a proof of his zeal as an idolator, he burnt one of his sons in sacrifice to Moloch. He dealt with familiar spirits, and had intercourse with devils; and, what is more awful still, he filled Jerusalem, from one end to the other, with the innocent blood of God's saints. How great must the forbearance and long-suffering of God have been to this wicked wretch, or he had been cut down in the height of his wickedness! But, wonder, O heavens, and be astonished, O earth! that one so full of mischief and enmity to all righteousness should be a vessel of mercy — an heir of glory! For notwithstanding his wickedness, God's all-conquering grace reached Manasseh's heart, laid him prostrate in the dust, and made him an humble supplicant before the God of his fathers. The Lord was entreated of him, and blessed him with the pardon of all his sins, because He was not willing that he should perish, but come to repentance.

See the long-suffering of God to Mary Magdalene, that sinful and vile woman who was possessed of seven devils, being a harlot, living in the filth of sin and abomination. Had it not been for the Lord's forbearance, she would have sunk in sin to rise no more. "But God, who is rich in mercy, for his great love wherewith he loved (her), even when (she) was dead in trespasses and sins," could not give Mary up; for she had a place in His heart. In due time He brought her, by the power of His grace to His blessed feet, in Simon's house; where with a broken and contrite heart, she washed His feet with her tears, and wiped them with the hair of her head; and the Lord said of her, "Her sins, which are many, are forgiven." What a proof is this that the Lord was not willing that Mary should perish, but come to repentance!

I would also call your attention to the Samaritan woman. It is said that Christ "must needs go through Samaria," because there were some of His people there, and the set time to call them by His grace was come. Now there was a woman who was to be the firstfruits of His grace amongst the Samaritans, who had had five husbands, and the man she was then living with was not her husband but they were living together in fornication. You see, the Lord was long-suffering towards this woman, till the time He had appointed to meet her at Jacob's well, to prove to her and to others that, sinful as she was, He was not willing that she should perish. Therefore, He gave her His grace which was in her heart as a well of living water, springing up into everlasting life. (John 4.)

We also behold the long-suffering of God towards Zacchaeus, the publican. Publicans in the days of Christ were collectors of the king's tribute or tax, and were generally looked upon as oppressive thieves and pickpockets, for they were in the habit of demanding more from the people than was Caesar's due, and by this means, enriching themselves. Zacchaeus was one of this sort, and to gratify his curiosity he climbed into a tree; but our Lord, to magnify the riches of His grace in one so vile, called him down, saying, "Zacchaeus, make haste and come down." The grace of our Lord Jesus Christ entered into his heart and brought him down. How evident it is that the grace of God makes men honest and benevolent; for no sooner had Zacchaeus come down the tree than he said to the Lord., "The half of my goods I give to the poor; and if I have taken any thing from any man by false accusation, I restore him fourfold." As a further proof that the Lord was not willing that he should perish, He said to him, "This day is salvation come to this house, forsomuch as he also is a son of Abraham. For the Son of man is come to seek and to save that which was lost." (Luke 19.)

We have another great proof of the long-suffering of God in Saul of Tarsus. He was a pharisee, and as touching the righteousness of the law, he was blameless in his own eyes; but there never was a more inveterately malicious enemy to Jesus of Nazareth and His humble followers than this Saul. He was mad against the church of God. He consented to the death of Stephen, and held the raiment of them that slew him. He made havoc of the saints, entering into every house and hailing men and women, committed them to prison, and compelled them to blaspheme the name of that Jesus on whom their hope for heaven depended. He breathed out threatening and slaughter against the disciples of Jesus, and went to the high-priest, and desired of him letters of authority that he might go to Damascus and bring the few that were there who called upon the name of the Lord, and have them bound fast as prisoners at Jerusalem.

This was Saul's free will, and it was carrying him as fast as possible towards hell, and it would have engulfed him there, but for free grace, which plucked him as a brand out of the fire, being a chosen vessel of mercy. The Lord, that He might magnify the riches of His grace in the salvation of the chief of sinners, suffered him to go near to Damascus, but not to enter in, the time being now come for Saul to be called by grace. And Jesus said to him, "Saul, Saul, why persecutest thou me? It is hard for thee to kick against the pricks." Down the rebel fell in the dust, and Jesus slew the enmity of his heart and made him willing to be anything or nothing, that Christ might be all in all. What a display of the grace and power of Christ shines forth in the conversion of Saul, and of the power of Christ resting upon him to fit and qualify him to preach that gospel he had laboured to destroy. From this time to his dying day, nothing but free grace and a dying Jesus's love would do for him; and he is now wearing his crown of glory in heaven, and shouting "Victory, through the blood of the Lamb."

I will refer you to another character we have left upon record, in whom the long-suffering of God shines forth, and truly this crowns all the rest. It is the thief upon the cross, in whom we have a display, not only of the long-suffering of God, but of His discriminating grace. There were two thieves crucified with Christ, one on the right hand and the other on the left; and these two thieves were both in one condition — both born in sin, going from their mother's womb speaking lies; both breakers of the law of God, which says, "Thou shalt not steal;" both a pest to society, breakers of the law of the land, and in consequence of which the civil sword of justice would not suffer them to live. They were both persecutors of Christ, for Matthew tells us that the "thieves also which were

11

crucified with him cast the same in his teeth" as the infuriated multitude did; and Mark says "*they* reviled him." So you see, in all these things they were both on a level, and both deserved to die and be damned. But see how the doctrine of election shines! One is taken to paradise, and the other is righteously left to perish in his sins; for our God "will have mercy on whom he will have mercy, and he will have compassion on whom he will have compassion." Behold then the long-suffering of God towards this guilty wretch. He is suffered to go on in his sins until he is brought into the jaws of death, as a malefactor, "hell from beneath being moved to meet him at his coming." But grace, triumphant grace even at the eleventh hour, plucks him out of the fire, because the Lord was not willing that he should perish, but His will was to take him with Him to heaven, as a trophy of His redeeming love and mercy. Therefore he said unto him, "To-day shalt thou be with me in paradise."

If we come down to more modern times, we may see the long-suffering of God towards John Bunyan, the tinker, who was so notoriously wicked that he became a byword amongst his neighbours. But the Lord was not willing that he should perish, but be brought to repentance and to flee from the city of destruction, as he sets it forth in his inimitable *"Pilgrim's Progress,"* and also in his *"Grace Abounding to the Chief of Sinners."*

We might also notice John Newton, whose praise is in all the churches, and whose hymns are sometimes sung with grace and melody in our hearts to the Lord. Behold this African blasphemer (as he styles himself) on the coasts of Africa, far off from God by wicked works, and far from his native shore. But the pitying eye of mercy saw him, and brought him back to his native land. During the time of a storm at sea, eternal things were laid with a solemn weight upon his mind, and in due time he was raised up to blow the silver trumpet of the everlasting gospel in the great metropolis of our land.

But, let us look to ourselves, and to the hole of the pit whence we were digged, and behold the state we were in. Were we not bent and determined to go in the lusts of our flesh, fulfilling the desires of the flesh and of the mind? Were we not by nature the children of wrath, even as others? I can speak for myself, and to my shame I would say it, never was a youth more determined to go on in sin than I was. I had a parent who feared the Lord and walked in His ways, and who desired to bring his children up in the way that they should go. But when I was compelled to go with him to the house of God, I cursed him in my heart. Had it been left to me and my free-will, I should have gone on in sin, and lived and died an enemy to God, till I had lifted up my eyes in hell. But the Lord was not willing that I should perish; for when I was about fifteen years of age, He was graciously pleased to put His fear into my heart, which was as a fountain of life to depart from the snares of death; and having obtained help of God, I have continued to this day, and am not without hope that the Lord will continue to hold me up, and be my God and guide even unto death and eternal glory.

Many of the Lord's family, after they have been called by divine grace, have been led to look back at the hair-breadth escapes they have had, and to admire and adore the kind and watchful care of the Lord over them, when they had no thought or care for themselves, and to sing with the poet —

> But see how heaven's indulgent care
> Attends their wanderings here and there;
> Still hard at heel where'er they stray,
> With pricking thorns to hedge their way.
>
> (Kent)

It is impossible for a vessel of mercy to be destroyed or to die before he is born again of God; for they are all predestinated to be called by God's grace, and to be conformed to the image of his Son, and are "afore prepared unto glory."

(ii). We now come to show that the Lord is long-suffering to His people, *after they are called by divine grace.*

We who see and feel our own weakness and daily failings and infirmities know that if the Lord were to lay righteousness to the line and judgment to the plummet and deal with us according to our sins, we should be swept away. But we rejoice that the Lord has proclaimed Himself to be "merciful and gracious, long-suffering, and abundant in goodness and truth." It is said that He "delights in mercy," and that He will be merciful to the unrighteousness of his people, and their sins and iniquities will he remember no more.

The Lord was long-suffering to David, the man after His own heart. We behold in him the heinous crimes of adultery and murder. Well might he cry out, "If thou, LORD, shouldst mark iniquity, O Lord, who shall stand? But there is forgiveness with thee, that thou mayest be feared." This David knew by experience, the Lord having put away his sin; for he says, "But thou, O Lord, art a God full of compassion, and gracious, long-suffering, and plenteous in mercy and truth." (Ps. 86. 15.)

Poor backsliding Peter, who denied his Lord and Master with oaths and curses, might well include himself among the "us-ward" in our text, to whom the Lord is long-suffering.

Jeremiah knew something of the long-suffering of God, for he says, "It is of the LORD'S mercies that we are not consumed, because his compassions fail not. They are new every morning: great is thy faithfulness." (Lam. 3. 22, 23.)

The Lord was long-suffering towards Ephraim, who was as a "cake not turned," and therefore good for nothing. He was as a bullock unaccustomed to the yoke, and instead of being a pleasant child he was a froward child. Nevertheless the Lord, though He spoke against him, could not give him up; for He says, "I do earnestly remember him still; therefore my bowels are troubled for him. I will surely have mercy upon him" (Jer. 31. 20.) How shall I give thee up, Ephraim? how shall I deliver thee, Israel? how shall I "make thee as Admah? how shall I set thee as Zeboim?" — two cities that were built upon the plains of Sodom and Gomorrah, which the Lord had overthrown. (Hos. 11. 8.) But He cannot consume His people, for they are "engraven on the palms of his hands, and their walls are continually before him." For their comfort He has said, "I am the Lord, I change not, therefore ye sons of Jacob are not consumed." So that He will not execute the fierceness of His anger; He will not return to destroy Ephraim; for He is "God, and not man; the Holy One in the midst of thee."

From these passages, you will see that such is the love of the Lord to His people, that none can turn it away from them; for after all their backslidings, He says, "Turn O backsliding children, . . for I am married unto you." (Jer. 3. 14.) Whatever men may say against this doctrine, telling us that it leads to sin, and so forth, we know the truth to be that the more we enjoy of it, the more we hate sin and love holiness. It constrains us to obedience to the precepts and exhortations of our God. It is by our fruit that we are known to be a peculiar people whom the Lord hath formed for Himself, to show forth His praise.

III

We now proceed to the third part of our subject, which is to show that **the Lord is not willing that any should perish.**

(1). That *Jehovah the Father is not willing that any should perish,* is evident from the following considerations:—

(i). *From the counsels of His will.* The Lord's will is not as ours; for we may have a will to do this or that, but for want of power we cannot accomplish that which we would.

The wicked cannot do the evil that they would; for that God that said to the raging sea, "Hitherto shalt thou come, but no further; and here shall thy proud waves be staid," hath set bounds to the passions of both men and devils; so that Abimelech could not take Sarah, the wife of Abraham, to his bed, nor could the wicked prophet Balaam go one whit behind the word of the Lord, to do more or less; neither could Satan move a hair's breadth against Job, but by divine permission.

The saints of God cannot do the good that they would; to will is present with them, but how to perform that which is good they find not; for the good that they would, they do not, but the evil that they would not, that they do. (Rom. 7. 18, 19.) They would live without sin if they could, but they cannot because of the depravity of their natures.

Not so with the Lord; "for our God is in the heavens; he hath done whatsoever he pleased." "Whatsoever the Lord pleased, that did he in heaven and in earth, in the seas, and all deep places." Nebuchadnezzar was necessitated to say, The Most High "doeth according to his will in the army of heaven, and among the inhabitants of the earth: and none can stay his hand, or say unto him, What doest thou?" (Dan. 4. 35.) Job proved Him to be "in one mind, and who can turn him? and what his soul desireth, even that he doeth." And Paul speaks of "the purpose of him who worketh all things after the counsel of his own will."

God the Father is not willing that any of His little ones should perish (Matt. 18. 14). He purposed or decreed in His own eternal mind that they shall be saved in Christ with an everlasting salvation. (Eph. 1. 11.) This is called "the mystery of his will, according to his good pleasure which he hath purposed in himself." (Eph. 1. 9.) It is also called "the purpose of God according to election," which shall stand. "My counsel

shall stand, and I will do all my pleasure." "The counsel of the
LORD standeth for ever, the thoughts of his heart to all
generations" (Ps. 33. 11). "There are many devices in a man's
heart; nevertheless the counsel of the LORD, that shall stand."

So you see, it is the will, counsel, and determination of
Jehovah the Father that His people should not perish, but be
brought to repentance here, and to glory hereafter. For "whom
he did predestinate them he also called; and whom he called,
them he also justified: and whom he justified, them he also
glorified." (Rom. 8. 30.) This passage has often, with great
propriety, been called the golden chain of salvation: and, it
rejoices my soul that a link of it cannot be broken, neither by
sin, the world, men, devils, death, nor hell, for these are all
vanquished foes —

> Our Jesus nailed them to his cross,
> And sung the triumph when he rose.

"Nay in all these things we are more than conquerors, through
him that loved us."

(ii).   We have another proof of the Father's unwillingness
that any of His people should perish *in the gift of His Son.*
"God so loved the world (which He was, in Christ,
reconciling to Himself), that he gave his only begotten Son,
that whosoever believeth in him should not perish, but have
everlasting life" (Jn. 3. 16.) "He . . . . spared not his own Son,
but delivered him up for us all, how shall he not with him also
freely give us all things?" (Ro. 8. 32.) "In this was manifested
the love of God towards us, because that God sent his only
begotten Son into the world, that we might live through him.
Herein is love, not that we loved God, but that he loved us, and
sent his Son to be the propitiation for our sins" (1 Jn. 4. 9, 10).
Paul's soul being directed into the love of the Father, as it
shines forth in the gift of his Son, joyfully exclaims "Thanks be
unto God for his unspeakable gift." Its greatness is such that no
tongue can describe nor thought conceive it.

The Father, speaking of this gift, says, I will "give thee for a
covenant of the people" (Isa. 42. 6); and when the Father gave
Christ in covenant, He did not give Him at random, but gave
Him to be the surety of His chosen people. For this people the
Lord Jesus Christ gave His bond, that in the fulness of time He
would redeem them to God by His blood, the blood of the

everlasting covenant. So He would open the way through which the love and mercy of the Father's heart could flow to guilty sinners such as we, in a way consistent with all His divine attributes, that He might be a just God and yet save His people in Christ.

(iii).   We have another proof of the Father's unwillingness that any of His people should perish, *in making them His adopted children.*

Adoption is an eternal act of the Father, in which He took His people into union with Himself in the covenant of grace, having "predestinated (them) to the adoption of children by Jesus Christ to himself, according to the good pleasure of his will." (Eph. 1. 5.) Thus predestinated, they are in due time called by God's grace; for He will "say to the north, Give up; and to the south, Keep not back; bring my sons from far, and my daughters from the ends of the earth." (Is. 43. 6.) You see, they are sons before they are called; and it is because they are sons that God sends forth the Spirit of His Son into their hearts, crying, "Abba, Father." (Gal. 4. 6.) Thus they were

> Predestinated to be sons,
>> Born by degrees, but chose at once;
> A new regenerated race,
>> To praise the glory of his grace.

(Watts)

The Holy Spirit bears witness with our spirit that we are the adopted children of God; "And if children, then heirs; heirs of God, and joint-heirs with Christ," of that inheritance which is "incorruptible, and undefiled, and that fadeth not away, reserved in heaven for us". This inheritance God's elect are predestinated by their heavenly Father to obtain. It is the kingdom our Lord speaks of saying, "Come, ye blessed of my Father, inherit the kingdom prepared for you from the foundation of the world." (Mt. 25. 34.) It is moreover evident from what our Lord said to the mother of Zebedee's children, that it is a kingdom prepared for a special people: "It shall be given to them for whom it is prepared of my Father." (Mt. 20. 23.) Paul speaks of "a building of God, an house not made with hands, eternal in the heavens." And our Lord informs us that in his "Father's house there are many mansions." We likewise

read that there are white robes, and palms of victory, and
crowns of glory, prepared and laid up in heaven for all that
love the Lord, and long for His appearing. (2 Tim. 4. 8.)

Thus, it is certain that there is a kingdom to be possessed, a
building in heaven to be inhabited, mansions to be occupied,
white robes to be clothed in, and crowns of glory to be worn.
And should any of the Lord's adopted children miss the
enjoyment of these glorious things given or bequeathed to them
by their heavenly Father in the covenant of grace and promised
to them in the word of God, the Holy Spirit blessing them with
an earnest of them in their hearts (Eph. 1. 14), the Lord would
be a disappointed God, defeated in His purposes and counsels.
But a defeated or disappointed God is not the God that made
the heavens, the earth, and the seas and all that therein is; nor is
He the God of the Bible, which tells us that heaven and earth
shall pass away, but not one jot or tittle of God's truth shall fall
to the ground, till all be fulfilled. Such a God will not do for
me; I never preached such a God, and trust I never shall. But
such is the Arminian's God, who, they say, wants to save all the
human race, but cannot. Moreover, if it be as they tell us, that
there are thousands in hell that the Lord wanted to be in
heaven, possessing those heavenly things of which we have
been speaking, does it not follow that the kingdom will be but
in part possessed, that there will be buildings or mansions
unoccupied, white robes unworn, and crowns laid up in heaven
and none to wear them? Such a confused system, we solemnly
and boldly discard, and I hope that the Lord will ever enable
me to trample it under my feet in the ministry of His word. For
"The ransomed of the LORD shall return, and come to Zion
with songs and everlasting joy upon their heads; they shall
obtain joy and gladness (yea, they shall possess the kingdom,
with all the blessings of glory and honour it contains), and
sorrow and sighing shall flee away." (Is. 35. 10.)

(2).   That *our Lord Jesus Christ is not willing that any of
His people should perish,* will appear evident from the
following considerations:—

(i).   *The covenant engagement of Christ.* The council of
peace was between the Father and the Word that was made
flesh. Hence Christ is said to be the Mediator of the better
covenant, which was established upon better premises; in
which covenant He became Surety or Bondman to the law and
justice of heaven for all the sins of His people. And when our

Lord gave that bond in covenant, He did it in full expectation that He would have the debt to pay, as all the sins or debts of His people were placed to His account. Here we see the love and compassion of the Redeemer's heart;

> This was compassion like a God,
> That when the Saviour knew
> The price of pardon was his blood,
> He pity ne'er withdrew.   (Watts)

This is the "everlasting covenant, ordered in all things, and sure," which was the joy of David's soul in the prospect of death and eternity, for it was all his salvation and all his desire (2. Sam. 23. 5.)

It was upon the ground of the covenant engagement of the Lord Jesus Christ, that the promises of His coming into the world were made. He was the seed of the woman which was to bruise the serpent's head. God promised Abraham that in His seed all the families or nations of the earth should be blessed. This was a promise of Christ, and Abraham believed it and rejoiced to see His day. (John 8. 58.) Christ was the bright and morning star that was to come out of Jacob (Num. 24. 17); and the Shiloh that should come when the sceptre was departed from Judah, unto whom the gathering of the people shall be. (Gen. 49. 10.) All these promises, and such as are of a like import, are founded upon the covenant engagement of Christ.

It was on the ground of this covenant engagement that the prophets were moved by the Holy Ghost to prophesy of the coming of Christ — the place where He should be born (Mic. 5. 2); the glory of His mysterious person as our Immanuel, the awful nature of His sufferings and death, and the triumph of His resurrection. (Isa. 53 and 63.) The patriarchs and prophets that lived before the coming of Christ believed these things, died in the faith of them, and went to heaven on the strength of them. And it is no disparagement to say that they went to heaven on the ground of credit; for had there been a failure in the payment of the debt they owed, which Christ had engaged in the fulness of time to pay, they would have sunk in darkness, horror, and despair. But, blessed be the name of the Lord, He failed not, nor was discouraged (Isa. 42. 4), but in due time paid the debt with His life and blood.

(ii).   Christ becoming incarnate for the express purpose of

saving His people, is another proof of His unwillingness that any of them should perish.

It being utterly impossible for us to save ourselves by any works of righteousness done by us, when we were utterly without strength, in due time Christ came. Not all the blood of bulls and goats that was spilt on Jewish altars could make a satisfactory atonement to divine justice for sin. Therefore Jesus in prophetic language said, "Lo, I come, in the volume of the book (of God's decrees and of the prophets) it is written of me, I delight to do thy will, O my God." (Ps. 40. 7, 8.) He threw by His radiant glory which He had with the Father "before the world was," and veiled His Godhead in a tabernacle of clay, being made of a woman, and made under the law, to redeem His people from the curse of the law, being made a curse for them. (Gal. 4. 4, 5; 3. 13.) He came to seek and to save the lost sheep of the house of Israel; and it is a faithful saying, and worthy of all acceptation that Christ came into the world to save the very chief of sinners. "Forasmuch then as the children are partakers of flesh and blood, he also himself likewise took part of the same, that through death he might destroy him that had the power of death, that is, the devil." Moreover He "hath brought life and immortality to light through the gospel." (Heb. 2. 14; 2 Tim. 1. 10.)

(iii). Christ's making an end of the sins of His people, and bringing in an everlasting righteousness for them, is another proof of His unwillingness that any of them should perish.

Christ is our spiritual scapegoat on whom all the sins of His people were laid, and He carried them into the land of forgetfulness, never more to return. (Lev. 16, 21, 22.) "All we like sheep have gone astray; we have turned every one to his own way; and the LORD hath laid on him the iniquity of us all. . . . . he was numbered with the transgressors; and he bare the sin of many, and made intercession for the transgressors" (Isa. 53. 6, 12). "He hath made him to be sin for us, who knew no sin (by nature or practice, being holy, harmless, undefiled, and separate from sin); that we might be made the righteousness of God in him" (2 Cor. 5. 21). "Once in the end of the world (the old dispensation) hath he appeared to put away sin by the sacrifice of himself." (Heb. 9. 26) He is said to have finished transgression, to have made an end of sin, to have made reconciliation for iniquity, to have brought in everlasting righteousness, and to have sealed up the vision (of Jehovah in

His ancient councils), and fulfilled the prophecies." (Dan. 9. 24.)

O, my friends, Christ having made an end of sin and put it away, is a sweet doctrine; and it has often warmed and animated my soul. ". . . saith the Lord, the iniquity of Israel shall be sought for, and there shall be none; and the sins of Judah, and they shall not be found; for I will pardon them whom I reserve." (Jer. 50. 20.) How sweetly does the poet sing of this blessed riddance of sin —

> Now if we search to find our sins,
> Our sins can ne'er be found,
> Awake, our hearts, adore the grace
> That buries all our faults,
> That pardoning blood, that swells above
> Our follies and our thoughts.

Beloved, as our sins are thus put away, made an end of, and removed as far as the east is from the west — two opposites that can never come together — they cannot appear against us to condemn us. "There is therefore now no condemnation to them which are in Christ Jesus;" for our transgressions are blotted out as a thick cloud. Though they often appear to us of so aggravating a nature that they seem to be of a scarlet or crimson hue, yet, they being washed away by the blood of the Lamb, we shall be white as snow or as wool; though black in ourselves as the tents of Kedar, we are white and comely through the comeliness that He has put upon us. (Sol. 1. 5.) Not only are our sins absolved through the blood of the cross, but heaven is well pleased for the righteousness' sake of Christ, for He has "magnified the law and made it honourable" (Isa. 42. 21); and this righteousness God has imputed to us. (Rom. 4. 6.) The language of Paul is the prayer of every one that is born and taught of God: To "be found in him, not having mine own righteousness, which is of the law, but that which is through the faith of Christ, the righteousness which is of God by faith;" (Phil. 3. 9) and this righteousness is said to be "unto and upon all them that believe." So then, being complete in Christ, and accepted in the Beloved, "who of God is made unto us wisdom, and righteousness, and sanctification, and redemption," our safe standing for eternity is as we stand in Christ; and of Him we joyfully sing —

Jesus, thy blood and righteousness
  My beauty are, my glorious dress;
Midst flaming worlds, in these arrayed,
  With joy shall I lift up my head.

Bold shall I stand in that great day,
  For who aught to my charge shall lay,
While through thy blood absolved I am
  From sin's tremendous curse and shame?

(Zinzendorf)

(iv). That Christ is not willing that any of His people should perish, is moreover evident *from His willingness to die for them.*

When the hour drew nigh that Jesus was to be delivered into the hands of sinful men, to be arraigned at Pilate's bar, and crucified and slain, we find Him in the garden of Gethsemane, resisting unto blood, striving against sin. Judas, who betrayed Him, knowing the place where He was, (for Jesus oftentimes resorted thither with His disciples) went, with a band of men and officers, and entered the garden, having lanterns, and torches, and weapons to take Him. Here behold His willingness to die for His people. Instead of fleeing from them, bold as a lion He went forth to meet them, and said to them, "Whom seek ye? They answered him, Jesus of Nazareth. Jesus saith unto them, I am he." And (being confounded) they went backward and fell to the ground. "Then asked he them again, Whom seek ye? And they said, Jesus of Nazareth. Jesus answered, I have told you that I am he; if, therefore, ye seek me, let these go their way." (John 18. 1-8.)

In all this, we see the willingness of Jesus to lay down His life for his people. He said, "Therefore doth my Father love me, because I lay down my life, that I might take it again. No man taketh it from me, but I lay it down of myself. I have power to lay it down, and I have power to take it again." (John 10. 17, 18.) Again He said, "I am the good shepherd; the good shepherd giveth his life for the sheep." (John 10. 11.) And it is further evident from what our Lord says that all men are not His sheep: "Ye believe not, because ye are not of my sheep, as I said unto you. My sheep hear my voice, and I know them, and they follow me and I give unto them eternal life and they shall never perish." (Jn. 10. 26) For "when the Son of man shall come in his glory, and all the holy angels with him, then shall he sit upon the throne of his glory: and before him shall be gathered all nations, and he shall separate them one from another, as a shepherd divideth his sheep from the goats. And he shall set the sheep on his right hand, but the goats on the left." (Mt. 25. 32, 33.) For the sheep are the objects of the Father's everlasting, electing love, and the purchase of the blood of the great Shepherd. They are the *"us-ward,"* the *"any,"* and the *"all"* in our text, whom God will bring to repentance here and to eternal glory hereafter.

Our Lord bought His people at too dear a rate ever to suffer any of them to perish. Had "the most high God, possessor of heaven and earth," and all that therein is" (Gen. 14. 19), given the sun, moon, and stars, the gold and the silver, and the cattle upon a thousand hills, for the redemption of His people, the price would have been amazingly great, but infinitely insufficient to redeem them. And, great as such a price would have been, it is not to be in the least degree compared with the price that has been given — the precious blood of Christ. For Christ gave his life a ransom for many" (Matt. 20. 28); to wit, for as many as were ordained by the Father unto eternal life. Paul tells us that Christ "gave himself for us (mark this!) He gave Himself for our sins an offering and a sacrifice to God for a sweetsmelling savour; that he might redeem us from all iniquity, and purify unto himself a peculiar people, zealous of good works." (Gal. 1. 4; Eph. 5. 2; Tit. 2. 4.)

The pronoun *us,* my friends, in the above passages, accords with the *us* in our text; and behold how evident it is that He is not willing that any of them should perish; for, to secure our everlasting welfare, He became our Bondman, or Surety, in the covenant of grace, in the councils of eternity, in the fulness of time becoming incarnate, that He might save us from our sins, and deliver us from the wrath to come; putting away all our sins by the sacrifice of Himself, and bringing in an everlasting righteousness to justify us; giving Himself for us, that He might destroy death and him that had the power of death, that is, the devil; being the plague of death and the destruction of the grave; bringing life and immortality to light through the gospel; and being delivered for our offences, and raised again for our justification. "Who," therefore, "shall lay anything to the charge of God's elect? It is God that justifieth; who is he that condemneth? It is Christ that died; yea, rather, that is risen again; who is even at the right hand of the Father, who also maketh intercession for us;" and "because he lives, we shall live also." Yes, my brethren, our great High Priest has entered into heaven itself, now to appear in the presence of God for us, being exalted "far above all principality, and power, and might, and dominion, and every name that is named, not only in this world, but also in that which is to come: and having all things put under his feet, and being given to be the head over all things to the church." (Eph. 1. 21, 22.) He tells us that "all power is given him in heaven and in earth." As Mediator, He hath "power given him over all flesh, that he might give eternal life to as many as the Father hath given him."

So, my friends, it is clear, from the testimony of God, that the work of redemption is finished by Christ, and that all power is in His hands; therefore, He will have His people with Him in glory.

(3). *That the Holy Ghost, the third person in the adorable Trinity, is not willing that any of His people should perish,* is evident from the following particulars:-

(i). *That the Holy Ghost is God, and one with the Father and the immortal Word in the salvation and glorification of the church,* is clearly revealed: "There are three that bear record in heaven, the Father, the Word, and the Holy Ghost; and these three are one" (1 Jn. 5. 7); "Go ye therefore, and teach all nations, baptizing them in the name of the Father, and of the Son, and of the Holy Ghost." (Mt. 28. 19).

We have already proved that God the Father has a chosen people, whom He has "ordained unto eternal life," and that for this people Christ has "obtained eternal redemption." Nevertheless, who this people are none can tell except as the Holy Ghost makes them manifest; for there is no difference between them and the rest of the world while they are in an unregenerate state, as they walk "according to the course of this world, according to the prince of the power of the air, the spirit that now worketh in the children of disobedience: Among whom also we all had our conversation in times past, in the lusts of our flesh, fulfilling the desires of the flesh and of the mind; and were by nature the children of wrath (or wrathful dispositions) even as others." (Eph. 2. 2, 3.)

The Holy Ghost in regeneration takes possession of the hearts of His people, for we are said to be the temples of the Holy Ghost, and that the Spirit of God dwells in our hearts. Now where this Spirit is, there is life: "You hath he quickened who were dead in trespasses and sins." The soul that is thus made alive by the quickening influence of God's Spirit, can no longer go on in sin, nor walk the way of sinners; for the Lord says to such, "Come out from among them, and be ye separate, saith the Lord, and touch not the unclean thing; and I will receive you, and will be a Father unto you, and ye shall be my sons and daughters." (2 Cor. 6. 17, 18) "Because ye are not of the world, but I have chosen you out of the world, therefore the world hateth you." (Jn. 15. 19) "They think it strange that ye run not with them to the same excess of riot, speaking evil of you." (1 Pet. 4. 4.)

(ii). · The Holy Spirit's convincing His people of their lost, sinful state and condition is another proof of His unwillingness that any of them should perish.

Our Lord made us a promise of the Holy Spirit, and said that when He came, His first work would be to convince the world of sin, and of the righteousness of God in His law. (Jn. 16. 7-11). Hence it is by the law in the hands of the Spirit, that we receive the knowledge of our sinful state and condition before God. The commandment being brought home to the conscience by His power, we die to all hope of being saved on the ground of our own works, and we learn experimentally that by the deeds of the law there shall no flesh be justified in the sight of God; and if we are not taught by the Spirit to know ourselves, we can never know Christ, "whom to know is eternal life." We must know and feel that we are sick before we can be healed; our hearts must be wounded and broken before the great Physician can bind them up; we must see and feel our shame and nakedness before we can put on by faith the garment of salvation; we must see and feel our guilty, condemned state as sinners, before we can enjoy the pardoning love and efficacious blood of the Lamb; and we must experimentally know that we are lost and undone before we can enjoy our interest in the finished work of Christ. These things the Lord has joined together in the experience of His family, and they are things which the Holy Ghost teaches.

(iii). We have another proof of the Holy Spirit's unwillingness that any of His people should perish, in *His leading them to put all their trust and confidence in Christ.*

It is part of the Spirit's work to glorify Christ, by taking of the things of Christ, and showing them to His people. He leads them to see that Christ and Him crucified is just such a Saviour as we stand in need of, for "he is able also to save them to the uttermost that come unto God by him." Yea, it is said of Him, that "he *will* save," that "he came into the world to seek and to save that which was lost."

The blessed Spirit leads us to see such beauty and glory in Christ, that our souls are all athirst for Him. "As the hart panteth after the waterbrooks, so panteth my soul after thee, O God." There is none that can help us but the Lord, and under the Spirit's influence we are enabled to cast ourselves at His blessed feet, saying as Esther said, "If I perish, I perish;" for at Jesus' feet I will lie, and

> Should worlds conspire to drive me thence,
> Moveless and firm this heart shall lie;
> Resolved, for that's my last defence,
> If I must perish, there to die.

(Watts)

All we want, in such a state of mind, is to know for ourselves that we have "redemption through his blood, the forgiveness of sins, according to the riches of his grace"; but this we cannot enjoy, unless the Holy Spirit takes of the blood of atonement and applies it to our conscience, bearing witness with our spirit that we are the children of God. Then we can say with the apostle Paul, "I know whom I have believed (or trusted), and am persuaded that he is able to keep that which I have committed unto him against that day."

(iv). The certainty that the Holy Spirit will complete the work of grace in the hearts of His people, is another proof of his unwillingness that any of them should perish.

Paul, writing to the Philippians, says, "Being confident of this very thing, that he which hath begun a good work in you will perform it until the day of Jesus Christ." (Phil. 1. 6.) The Holy Ghost is the author of the work of grace in the hearts of His people, and where He begins, He carries on and completes His work. Yes, though the world, the flesh, and the devil oppose, the Lord's work in the hearts of His people shall go on, because "greater is he that is in you, than he that is in the world." (1 John 4. 4.) Hannah, in her song, says, "He will keep the feet of his saints." Peter tells us, we are "kept by the power of God, through faith unto salvation." Solomon says, though the just man fall seven times, he shall rise up again. David says, "The steps of a good man are ordered by the LORD: and he delighteth in his way. Though he fall, he shall not be utterly cast down, for the LORD upholdeth him with his hand." (Ps. 37. 23, 24.) It is likewise said, the righteous shall hold on his way, and he that has clean hands (of faith) shall wax stronger and stronger. They that wait upon the LORD shall renew their strength (they shall be strengthened by the Spirit's might in their inner man); they shall mount up with wings as eagles; they shall run and not be weary; and they shall walk and not faint." (Is. 40. 31.) The weaker in ourselves, the stronger in the Lord.

> The feeble saint shall win the day,
> Though death and hell obstruct the way.

We cannot conclude this part of our subject better than in the language of Paul: "In all these things we are more than conquerors through him that loved us. For I am persuaded." This is a soul-comforting and God-glorifying persuasion, founded upon the covenant engagement of our triune Jehovah — "that neither death, nor life, nor angels, nor principalities, nor powers, nor things present, nor things to come, nor height, nor depth, nor any other creature, shall be able to separate us from the love of God, which is in Christ Jesus our Lord." (Rom. 8. 37-39.)

As the body without the soul is dead, so that religion is but a dead form which has not the Spirit of God to begin it, maintain it, carry it on, and complete it in our eternal glorification.

IV

We now come to the fourth and last part of our subject, namely, that all should come to repentance.

In considering the doctine of repentance we will first show that there is a repentance spoken of in the Scriptures, of which we may be the subjects, and yet not be possessed of that which is connected with the salvation of the soul.

(1).   Such was the repentance of the Ninevites. The Lord commanded Jonah to go to Nineveh, that great city, and cry against it, for their wickedness was come up before Him. But Jonah rose up to flee to Tarshish, from the presence of the Lord. Nevertheless, the Lord brought him back again, and made him willing to go to Nineveh and preach the preaching that He bade him. Jonah entered this great city, and cried, in the name of the Lord, "Yet forty days, and Nineveh shall be

overthrown." But the people of Nineveh repented at the preaching of Jonah. Now this repentance was a *national* one, for *national* crime, and it was universal, from the king on the throne to the meanest beggar; and the Lord, as the God of nature seeing their works, that they turned from their wicked ways, repented of the evil (or revoked the threatened judgment) that He had said He would do unto them, and He did it not (Jonah 4.)

(2). There is also a repentance, commonly called *legal,* which arises from fear of the punishment and shame connected with sin. We have an instance of this in Judas. The evangelist Matthew tells us that "Judas, which had betrayed him, when he saw that he was condemned, repented himself, and brought again the thirty pieces of silver to the chief priests and elders, saying, I have sinned in that I have betrayed the innocent blood.. . . ." (Mt. 27. 3, 4.) This did not arise from a principle of hatred to sin and love to God and holiness, but from a slavish fear of the just judgments of God which he saw hanging over his guilty head, ready to burst upon him, because he had betrayed innocent blood. His sorrow was the sorrow of the world, which worketh death. (2 Cor. 7. 10) It is thus with the malefactor who has broken the law of his country and is tried and condemned for his crime. He repents, grieves, and mourns, not because he hates vice and loves virtue, but because of the punishment and disgrace he has brought upon himself. Only let him loose again upon the public, and it is most likely he will do the same again. So with the drunkard. When he has spent his money and injured his character, circumstances, and family, how readily he says he repents, and will do so no more; but let him have some money in his pocket, and be exposed to temptation, and he is gone again, thereby making good the proverb, "The repenting drunkard never mends." His resolutions are merely made in the flesh, and therefore will not stand.

(3). The repentance spoken of in our text is very different to those we have been describing. It is gospel repentance, commonly called *evangelical,* being one of those spiritual blessings our heavenly Father has given us in Christ in the covenant of grace (Eph. 1. 3); and it is given to the Lord's covenant people by Christ, because He is "not willing that any of them should perish, but come to repentance." The apostle Peter confirms this fact: "Him hath God exalted with his right

hand to be a Prince and Saviour, for to give repentance to Israel, and forgiveness of sins." (Ac. 5. 31.) You see, how clear it is that Christ is the giver of true repentance to His people Israel, as well as the forgiveness of sins. In Acts 10 and 11, we have an interesting account of Peter being directed by the Lord to go and preach the gospel amongst the Gentiles; and he was not disobedient to the heavenly vision, but went with the men to the house of Cornelius, and preached unto them Christ and Him crucified, and the resurrection of Christ from the dead. And God gave testimony to the word of His grace; for these Gentiles repented, believed, and were baptized. When Peter returned to Jerusalem, his brethren that were of the circumcision blamed him for going amongst the Gentiles; but Peter rehearsed the matter from the beginning, and expounded it by order to them; and when the apostles and brethren heard the great things God had done for the Gentiles, they glorified God, saying, "Then hath God also to the Gentiles granted repentance unto life." From this, it is evident that true repentance towards God is the special grant of Heaven; and none ever did, nor ever will, possess this blessing but the sheep of Christ, unto whom He gives it, and "they shall never perish." (John 10. 28.)

The doctrine of repentance and remission of sins was to be preached in the name of Jesus among all nations, beginning at Jerusalem; because the "election of grace" that are to be made its happy partakers are scattered abroad amongst all the nations of the earth. John the Baptist preached the doctrine of repentance to the Jews who were looking for justification on the ground of their own works and their being the children of Abraham. Thus he laid the axe to the root of the tree, and ministerially hewed down all their false props, showing them the necessity of repentance towards God, and faith in the Messiah. (Luke 3. 2-10.)

"After that John was put in prison, Jesus came into Galilee, preaching the gospel of the kingdom of God, and saying, The time is fulfilled and the kingdom of God is at hand: repent ye, and believe the gospel." (Mark 1. 14-15.) "He called them to repent, not only of their former sins and vicious course of life, but of their bad principles and tenets concerning the temporal kingdom of the Messiah; concerning merit and free will, justification by the works of the law, and salvation by their obedience to the ceremonies of it, and the traditions of the

160 GRACE ALONE

elders: these he exhorts them to change their sentiments about, and to relinquish them, and give in to the gospel scheme; which proclaims liberty from the law, peace, pardon, and righteousness by Christ, and salvation and eternal life by the free grace of God." (John Gill, *Exposition of the New Testament* — Mark 1. 15.)

When our Lord was told by the Jews, of the Galileans whose blood Pilate had mingled with the sacrifices, and of those eighteen upon whom the tower in Siloam fell and slew them, it being evident that they supposed those characters who suffered were sinners above the rest of mankind, He undeceived them, by preaching to them the necessity of even *their* repentance, saying to them, "I tell you, Nay; but, except *ye* repent, ye shall all likewise perish." (Luke 13. 1-5.)

We are all sinners against a just and holy God, and we must be brought to repent of our sins before God, and confess them with a broken and a contrite heart, as David did, when he said, "Against thee, thee only, have I sinned, and done this evil in thy sight." If we are thus enabled to confess our sins, God "is faithful and just to forgive us our sins, and to cleanse us from all unrighteousness."

On the day of Pentecost, Peter stood up at Jerusalem, and preached Christ and Him crucified, charging the death of Christ upon His murderers: "Him, being delivered by the determinate counsel and foreknowledge of God, ye have taken, and by wicked hands have crucified and slain." He then goes on to preach to them the resurrection of Christ from the dead, and proves the doctrine of the resurrection from what was written in the Psalms concerning Him; and when they heard this, "they were pricked in their heart, and said unto Peter and to the rest of the apostles, Men and brethren, what shall we do? Then Peter said unto them, Repent, and be baptized every one of you in the name of Jesus Christ for the remission of sins." (Acts 2. 23; 37, 38.)

The doctrine of repentance Paul preached to the men of Athens, when he saw the inscription to the unknown God whom they ignorantly worshipped. He told them that there was one only living and true God, "That made the world and all things therein. . . . in whom we live, and move, and have our being;" and this God he proves to be the only object of worship and adoration. "And the times of this ignorance God winked at; but now commandeth all men every where to repent." (Acts

17. 24. 28, 30.) As Dr. Gill's views on this passage are fully expressive of my own, I will give them in his own words: "That is, he has given orders that the doctrine of repentance, as well as remission of sins, should be preached to all nations, to Gentiles as well as Jews; and that it becomes them to repent of their idolatries, and turn from their idols, and worship the one only living and true God; and though for many hundreds of years God had neglected them, and sent no messengers nor messages to them to acquaint them with His will, and to show them their follies and mistakes; yet now He has sent His apostles unto them, to lay before them their sins, and call them to repentance. And to stir them up to this, the apostle informs them of the future judgment in the following verse. Repentance being represented as a command does not suppose it to be in the power of men, or contradict evangelical repentance, being the free-grace gift of God; but only shows the need men stand in of it, and how necessary and requisite it is: and when it is said to be a command to all, this does not destroy its being a special blessing of the covenant of grace to some, but points out the sad condition that all men are in as sinners, and that without repentance they must perish. And, indeed, all men are obliged to natural repentance for sin, though to all men the grace of evangelical repentance is not given." *(Exposition of the New Testment* — Acts 17. 30.)

The necessity of repentance being thus preached by John, the harbinger of Christ, and even by our Lord Himself, as well as His apostles, and seeing that it is an important branch of divine truth, it is our duty to insist upon it, as well as upon the new birth and faith in Christ; for as we cannot enter into the kingdom of heaven if we are not born again of the Holy Spirit, neither can we enjoy the remission of our sins unless we be made true penitents.

It is by faith that we enjoy our interest in the salvation of Christ. Regeneration, repentance, and faith are all needful as graces of the Holy Spirit, and without the enjoyment of them we cannot be saved. Nevertheless, they are not our salvation, but the fruits and effects of it. "Faith and repentance went together in Christ's ministry (Mark 1. 15), and so they did in the ministry of John the Baptist (Acts 19. 4), and likewise in that of the apostle Paul, for he testified 'both to the Jews, and also to the Greeks, repentance toward God, and faith toward our Lord Jesus Christ.' (Acts 20. 21.) When they preached that men should repent, it does not from hence follow that they have a power to repent of themselves; for such is the condition of man by nature, that they neither see their need of repentance, and their hearts are so hard and obdurate that they cannot work themselves up to it, or work it in them and exercise it. This requires the powerful and efficacious grace of God to produce it, and it is a gift of His grace; and if He give the means and not the grace of repentance itself, it will never appear. But the apostles' preaching that men should repent, shows that they were in such a state as to need it, and how necessary it was for them to have it, seeing without it they must perish; and such a ministration is proper to awaken the minds of them to a sense of the need of it, and to direct them to Christ, who is exalted to give it, as well as the remission of sins." (*John Gill, Exposition of the New Testament* — Mark 6. 12.)

True evangelical repentance is a godly sorrow for sin arising from a principle of love to God; so that though there were no hell or punishment connected with sin, the soul that is born of God would hate and abhor sin, as Job did when he said, "I abhor myself, and repent in dust and ashes." We may also add the testimony of Ephraim, who said, "Surely after that I was turned I repented; and after that I was instructed, I smote upon my thigh: I was ashamed, yea, even confounded, because I did bear the reproach of my youth." (Jer. 31. 19.) From this passage, it is evident that Ephraim did not repent till he was turned, or changed by God's grace; and being taught of God what a guilty sinner he was both by nature and by practice, he smote upon his thigh, "as expressive of sorrow for sin, after a godly sort of indignation at it; and shame and confusion for it, and also of astonishment at the mercy, forbearance. and long-suffering of God." (Gill, *in loc*) He was ashamed of himself and of his vain and sinful thoughts, words, and ways, and was confounded, feeling the depravity of his nature and bearing the reproach (or iniquity) of his youth.

Sin is a burden to the true Christian, and it makes him cry out with Paul, "O wretched man that I am! who shall deliver me from the body of this death?" or, like the publican, he falls down at the Lord's feet, and his prayer is, "God be merciful to me a sinner." He smites upon his breast, intimating that it is not only his outward sins that he is confessing before God, but his heart sins arising from the depravity of his nature; for he feels himself to be altogether as an unclean thing, and that "the whole head is sick, and the whole heart faint, from the sole of the foot even to the head there is no soundness in it; but wounds, and bruises, and putrefying sores." Where there is true penitence, there will be a hatred of garments spotted with the flesh. True godly sorrow for sin evidences itself in a forsaking of it: "He that covereth his sins shall not prosper: but whoso confesseth and forsaketh them shall have mercy." (Prov. 23. 13.)

Therefore, if we would find a true penitent, we must not go amongst the men of the world, who are given up to carnal pleasures, for we cannot find him where they delight to meet. The theatre, the ballroom, the race-ground, the tavern, and such like, are not places where the true penitent sinner can live, move, and be happy, no more than fish can live out of water. So that to find a broken-hearted sinner, we must look where weeping Mary was, namely, at Jesus's feet; for there is no place so suitable to his state of mind, as to lie low in the dust at the feet of Mercy. "They shall ask the way to Zion with their faces thitherward, saying, Come and let us join ourselves to the LORD in a perpetual covenant that shall not be forgotten." (Jer. 50. 5.) The tabernacles of the Lord are amiable to such, and their "soul longeth, yea, even fainteth for the courts of the LORD. . . . . For a day in thy courts is better than a thousand." The penitent sinner would "rather be a doorkeeper in the house of my God than to dwell in the tents of wickedness." (Ps. 84. 1-10.)

"If any man be in Christ, he is a new creature; old things are passed away; behold all things are become new." Such a man has new views of himself as a guilty, weak, and helpless worm, and of God, as a just and holy God, that will by no means clear the guilty; for mercy cannot shine forth at the expense of justice. He has new views of Christ, in whom mercy and truth are met together, righteousness and peace have kissed each other. Sin never appears in such hateful colours and so odious a light as when we behold it laid on Christ, and are led by the Holy Spirit to consider Him that endured such contradiction of sinners against Himself, resisting unto blood, striving against sin. We behold Him by faith nailed to the accursed tree. His hands and feet bruised with the rugged nails: "Surely he hath borne our griefs, and carried our sorrows; yet we did esteem him stricken, smitten of God, and afflicted. But he was wounded for our transgressions, he was bruised for our iniquities: the chastisement of our peace was upon him; and with his stripes we are healed." It pleased the Lord to bruise Him, and make His soul an offering for sin, that guilty sinners might be saved; and He has promised to "pour upon the house of David, and upon the inhabitants of Jerusalem, the spirit of grace and of supplications; and they shall look upon me whom they have pierced, and they shall mourn for him, as one mourneth for his only son, and shall be in bitterness for him, as one that is in bitterness for his first born." When we are led by faith to look upon Christ, whom we with our sins have pierced, we do not lay all the blame upon the wicked Jews, but feel that we are equally guilty. As Hart sings —

> They nailed him to the accursed tree;
> (They did, my brethren so did we);
> The soldier pierced his side, 'tis true;
> But we have pierced him through and through.

The sorrow that arises from a view of the sufferings and death of Christ is that godly sorrow which "worketh repentance to salvation not to be repented of." There is a solemn joy mingled with this godly sorrow that cannot be fully described. None ever enjoyed it but those who know Christ for themselves, "and the power of his resurrection, and the fellowship of his sufferings, being made conformable unto his death." Dr. Watts was very blessedly led into this godly sorrow for sin when he composed this hymn —

> Alas! and did my Saviour bleed?
> And did my Sovereign die?
> Would he devote that sacred head
> For such a worm as I?
>
> But drops of grief can ne'er repay
> The debt of love I owe:
> Here, Lord, I give myself away;
> 'Tis all that I can do.

To conclude. This is the repentance to the enjoyment of which the Lord will have His people come. Therefore, in His own time and way, He gives it to them; and as it is one of the fruits or graces of the Spirit, He works it in their hearts; for He "works in them to will and to do of His good pleasure." From Him is their fruit found; and to every soul that He gives this grace of repentance, He will give eternal glory, because He is not willing that any of them should perish.

As there are many passages which the advocates for the universal scheme bring forward to support their hypothesis besides that which we have had under consideration, I will proceed to examine a few of them.

The first to which I would call your attention is Ezek. 18. 30-32: "Therefore I will judge you, O house of Israel, every one according to his ways, saith the Lord GOD." In order to understand these words aright, we must take into consideration the relation in which Israel stood to the Lord. The Lord declared to Abram that He would make of him a great nation, and that He would be their God and King as a nation, and their Legislator or Lawgiver. This covenant they often brake, and worshipped idols, following after other gods, and He here threatens to judge them according to their evil ways, telling them if they did not repent, and turn themselves from all their transgressions, their iniquity would become their ruin. This repentance is *national*, for national crime, the same as that of the Ninevites. — "Cast away your transgressions, whereby ye have transgressed." That is, cast away your idols, and idol worship, which are an abomination unto you, and a trespass against me. — "And make you a new heart and a new spirit; for why will ye die, O house of Israel?" By their making them a new heart we learn that they had an idolatrous heart, and were given up to a spirit of idolatry. The Lord calls upon them, as His rational creatures, to have a heart to fear and reverence Him as their God and King, who had done so much for them as a nation. — "For I have no pleasure in the death of him that dieth, saith the Lord GOD; wherefore turn yourselves, and live ye." That the Lord has no pleasure in the death or overthrow of a city or nation, is evident from the many threatenings and exhortations that He has given in His word, for "He doth not afflict willingly nor grieve the children of men." (Lam. 3. 33.)

How different from this are the stipulations of the covenant of grace and salvation! "Behold, the days come saith the Lord, when I will make a new covenant with the house of Israel, ... not according to the covenant that I made with their fathers, when I brought them out of the land of Egypt, which covenant they brake; but this is the covenant that I will make with them; a new heart will I give them, and a new spirit will I put within them; and I will take away the stony heart out of their flesh. I will put my fear into their hearts, and they shall not depart from me. I will put my law in their inward parts, and write it in their hearts, and will be their God, and they shall be my people. For I will be merciful to their unrighteousness and their sins and their iniquities will I remember no more." (Heb. 8. 8, 9; Ezek. 36. 26; Jer. 32. 40; Heb. 8. 10-12.)

Nothing is more common in the mouths of the Arminians, and even of some of our professed modern Calvinists, than the words of our Lord: "O Jerusalem, Jerusalem, thou that killest the prophets, and stonest them which are sent unto thee, how often would I have gathered thy children together, even as a hen gathereth her chickens under her wings, and ye would not!" (Matt. 23. 37.) This they bring forward to oppose the doctrine of election and irresistible grace, and to vindicate the free will of man. But the plain and true sense of the passage is this: Christ is addressing the rulers and governors of Jerusalem, who killed the prophets and stoned such as were sent unto them by God. These rulers are called fathers, because they had the care and government of the inhabitants of Jerusalem, as a father has of his children. And observe, it is not said, "How often would I have gathered *you*, and *ye* would not," as the passage is so often misquoted; but, "How often would I have gathered *thy children*, . . . and *ye* (rulers) would not!" "For ye shut up the kingdom of heaven against men; for ye neither go in yourselves, neither suffer ye them that are entering to go in." (Matt. 23. 13.)

The gathering here spoken of is the gathering of the people under the ministry of the word, that Christ might instruct them in the knowledge of Himself as the Messiah. "The will of Christ to gather these persons is not to be understood of His divine will, or of His will as God, 'for who hath resisted his will?' — this cannot be hindered nor made void — 'he hath done whatsoever he pleased,' — but of His human will, or His will as a man, which, though not contrary to the divine will, but subordinate to it, yet not always the same with it, nor always fulfilled." For instance, when the Lord was praying in the garden, we hear Him say, "Father, if it be possible, let this cup pass from me; nevertheless not my will (as a man), but thine, be done." As a man, He wept at the grave of Lazarus, and over Jerusalem, when He saw the judgments that hung over her head. In the passage under consideration, He "speaks as a man and minister, and expresses human affection for the inhabitants of Jerusalem, and an humane wish for their temporal good. Besides, this will of gathering the Jews to Him was in Him, and expressed by Him, at certain several times by intervals, and therefore, He says, 'How often would I have gathered,' whereas, the divine will is one continued, invariable, and unchangeable will; is always the same, and never begins nor ceases to be; and to which such an expression as this is inapplicable; and, therefore, this passage of Scripture does not contradict the absolute and sovereign will of God in the distinguishing acts of it in election and effectual calling." (John Gill, *Exposition* — Matt. 23. 37.)

We shall see the difference between the human feelings of Christ, as manifested in the above case, and the Spirit of Christ, if we turn to Luke 10. 17-20. The disciples rejoiced that the spirits were subject to them through the name of the Lord; but Jesus said to them, "Rejoice not, that the spirits are subject unto you; but rather rejoice, because your names are written in heaven." And in verse 21 it is said, "In that hour Jesus rejoiced in spirit, and said, I thank thee, O Father, Lord of heaven and earth, that thou hast hid these things from the wise and prudent, and hast revealed them unto babes; even so, Father, for so it seemed good in thy sight." There is and must be a divine harmony in the word of God, between these two passages as well as the rest; and to me it appears impossible to ascertain their harmony on any other ground than the distinction there is between the human and the divine nature of Christ.

It must be clear to all, from the above statements that there is a distinction to be made between the feelings of humanity in the person of our Lord Jesus Christ, and that God who is a spirit; for our God, as God, is not the subject of those feelings and passions as we are: "My thoughts are not your thoughts, neither are your ways my ways, saith the LORD. For as the heavens are higher than the earth, so are my ways higher than your ways, and my thoughts than your thoughts." (Is. 55. 8, 9.)

In the controversy between James Hervey and John Wesley, the latter gentleman, in speaking against the doctrine of election, represents the Lord as being worse than man, inasmuch as the Lord according to election saves whom He will, and leaves the rest to perish in their sin. "But," says Wesley, "such are the benevolent feelings of men, that they would have all the human race of Adam saved." Thus he concludes that the conduct of God, in the predestination of His people, lays His compassion lower than the compassion of man; and to the eye of reason the argument appears somewhat plausible.

But how pointed, clear, and striking is Hervey's reply to this argument: "News is brought that the Prince George man-of-war, Admiral Broderick's own ship, is burnt and sunk, and above four hundred persons that were on board had perished. Six hours the flames prevailed, while every means was used to preserve the ship and crew, but all to no purpose. In the mean time, shrieks, and groans, bitter moaning, and piercing cries, were heard from every quarter. Raving despair and even madness presented themselves in a variety of forms. Some ran to and fro, distracted with terror, not knowing what they did or what they should do. Others jumped overboard from all parts, and, to avoid the pursuits of one death, leaped into the jaws of another. Those unhappy wretches who could not swim were obliged to remain upon the wreck, though flakes of fire fell upon their bodies. Soon the masts went away, and killed numbers. Those who were not killed thought themselves happy to get upon the floating timber. Nor yet were they safe; for the fire, having communicated itself to the guns, which were loaded and shotted, they swept multitudes from their last refuge."

Mr. Hervey, having related this circumstance, makes a solemn appeal to Mr. Wesley: "What say you, sir, to this dismal narrative? does not your heart bleed? would you have stood by and denied your succour, if it had been in your power to help? would not you have done your utmost to prevent the fatal catastrophe? Yet the Lord saw this extreme distress; He heard their piteous moans; He was able to save them, yet withdrew His assistance. Now, because you would gladly have succoured them if you could, and God almighty could but would not send them aid, will you therefore conclude that you are above your Lord, and that your loving-kindness is greater than His? I will not offer to charge any such consequence upon you. I am persuaded you abhor the thought."

The language of Peter, in the house of Cornelius the Gentile, is often brought forward in support of the universal scheme: "Then Peter opened his mouth, and said, Of a truth I perceive that God is no respecter of persons; but in every nation he that

feareth him and worketh righteousness, is accepted with him."
(Acts 10. 34, 35).

From these words it is contended that the Lord does not
respect one man more than another; that if the sinner will
exercise the freedom of his will, and turn to God, and fear
Him, and work righteousness, the Lord will love him, and he
shall be saved; and this fearing the Lord and working
righteousness, is considered, either in whole or in part, to be
the ground of acceptance with God. Hence sinners, dead in sin,
are told that if they do these things, they will be saved; but if
they do them not, they will be damned. Thus they make it out
that salvation and damnation depend upon the works of the
creature; consequently, that the sinner is beforehand with
God. But how different are these statements to the tenor of
God's word! As an axe laid to the root of such tenets it hews
them down: "We love him, because he first loved us." "But
Esaias is very bold and saith, I was found of them that sought me
not; I was made manifest unto them that asked not after me."
"Ye have not chosen me, but I have chosen you, and ordained
you." "By grace are ye saved through faith; and that not of
yourselves, it is the gift of God; not of works, lest any man
should boast." "To him that worketh not, but believeth on him
that justifieth the ungodly, his faith (that is, Christ the object of
his faith) is counted for righteousness." Thus boasting is
excluded, not by the law of works, but, by the law of faith,
which lays the sinner in the dust, and crowns Jehovah Lord of
all in the salvation of His church.

When Peter said, "I perceive that God is no respecter of
persons. . . " it is evident that he was convinced of the error
that the Jews and even the apostles themselves had been in,
namely, that the Lord respected the Jews more than the
Gentiles. The sheet let down from heaven, "wherein were all
manner of four-footed beasts of the earth, and wild beasts, and
creeping things, and fowls of the air," fully convinced Peter
than God had of His elect family among all the nations of the
earth, and that the distinction of Jew and Gentile, circumcision
or uncircumcision, bond or free, male or female, were all done
away in Christ, and that the church of God of whatever nation,
or tongue, or people, are all one in Christ Jesus, who has
broken down the middle wall of partition, that He might be His
church's all and in all.

In every nation, then, under heaven, he that fears God, and, under the influence of the Spirit of God, works righteousness, is accepted of Him; but it is not our fearing God and working righteousness that is the ground or foundation of our acceptance with Him. Decidedly not; we are "accepted in Christ the beloved" (Eph. 1. 6); We "are complete in him, which is the head of all principality and power" (Col. 2. 10.) We must not look to anything done by us, nor to any of the graces of the Holy Spirit that are wrought in us, as the ground of acceptance in the sight of Jehovah, as a just and holy God; but to the person, blood, and righteousness of Christ; for it is in Him alone that the seed of Israel are justified, and shall glory. (Isa. 45. 25.) It is our fearing God and working righteousness that are the evidence of our acceptance with God; as it is written, "By their fruits ye shall know them." And when we have done all, we must count it but loss for the excellency of the knowledge of Christ Jesus our Lord, for whom Paul suffered the loss of all things, and counted them but dung, that he might win Christ, and be found in Him, complete and accepted.

I have often, with a solemn pleasure, admired Dr. Watts' hymn on this subject —

> Yes, and I must and will esteem
>   All things but loss for Jesus' sake:
> O may my soul be found in him,
>   And of his righteousness partake!
>
> The best obedience of my hands
>   Dares not appear before thy throne;
> But faith can answer thy demands
>   By pleading what my Lord has done.

Now may the blessing of almighty God, Father, Son, and Holy Ghost, accompany His word; and His shall be all the praise and the glory. Amen and amen.